MAXIMUM
MUSCLE

FACTORY SPECIAL MUSCLECARS

STEVE STATHAM

MBI Publishing
Company

First published in 2001 by MBI Publishing
Company, 729 Prospect Avenue, PO Box 1,
Osceola, WI 54020-0001 USA

The information in this book is true and complete
to the best of our knowledge. All recommendations
are made without any guarantee on the part of the
author or Publisher, who also disclaim any liability
incurred in connection with the use of this data or
specific details.

We recognize that some words, model names and
designations, for example, mentioned herein are
the property of the trademark holder. We use them
for identification purposes only. This is not an
official publication.

MBI Publishing Company books are also available
at discounts in bulk quantity for industrial or sales-
promotional use. For details write to Special Sales
Manager at Motorbooks International Wholesalers
& Distributors, 729 Prospect Avenue, PO Box 1,
Osceola, WI 54020-0001 USA.

Library of Congress Cataloging-in-Publication Data
Stathem, Steve.
    Maximum muscle : factory special muscle cars/
Steve Statham.
        p. cm.—(Muscle car color history)
    Includes index.
    ISBN 0-7603-0877-2 (pbk. : alk. paper)
        1. Muscle cars—United States—History. 2.
Automobiles, Racing. I. Title. II. MBI Publishing
Company muscle car color history.

    TL23.S653 2001
    629.228'0973—dc21   00-069103

Printed in China

On the front cover: The 1970 Ford Boss 302 and
the 1970 Plymouth Superbird were two of the
greatest specialized muscle cars ever built. The
Plymouth Superbird's distinctive front nose and rear
wing gave the car an enormous competitive
advantage. Bobby Isaac drove it to the NASCAR
Grand National championship in 1970. Only 1,920
Superbirds were built for the street, making it one
of the rarest Mopar musclecars ever made. It was
available with either a 375-horsepower 440 Super
Commando V-8 or the 425-horsepower 426 Hemi.
Like the Superbird, the Boss 302 produced similar
results. Parnelli Jones captured the 1970 SCCA
Trans-Am championship with the 302. For the
production car, Ford pulled out all the stops to
produce the best handling car possible. The
production car featured wide 60 series tires, large
spindles, braced shock towers, 0.72-inch front
sway bar, high-performance shocks, and stiff springs.

On the frontispiece: The AAR graphic was a badge
of distinction. It was fitted to Plymouth's Trans-Am
pony car, the AAR 'Cuda. The car contained a
high-revving 340 small-block V-8 fitted with three
two-barrel carbs that produced 290 horsepower.

On the title page: The Ford Thunderbolt was an
exceptionally fast drag car. This particular 427 V-8,
featured a high-rise manifold and experimental
hemi cylinder heads, cast in aluminum, and
developed by Mickey Thompson. *Mike Mueller photo*

On the back cover, top: The Mercury Cyclone
Spoiler II aerodynamic front fascia helped the car
slice the wind. The Dan Gurney edition carried a
blue and white color scheme. *Mike Mueller photo*
bottom: The 2000 Mustang Cobra R series
represents a return to the days of factory-built race
cars. The race-tuned engine, sky-high wing, and
massive hood bulge recall the days of lightweight
Galaxies and Thunderbolts. *SVT photo*

Edited by Paul Johnson
Designed by Bruce Leckie

CONTENTS

ACKNOWLEDGMENTS

As always, many people helped in the preparation of this book. I burned plenty of film on my own but couldn't photograph every cool car in the country, so I thank comrade-in-ink Mike Mueller for photos of Sam Pierce's 1962 Z11 Impala, Henry Hart's 1962 Super Duty Pontiac, David Gieger's 1964 Ford Thunderbolt, Roger Brink's 1966 W-30 Oldsmobile, Bill Jacobsen's 1969 Charger Daytona, and Randy Lewis' 1969 Mercury Cyclone Spoiler IIs. I also owe Californian Bob Tronolone gracious thanks for use of his period racing photos of Parnelli Jones, Peter Revson, Mark Donohue, Richard Petty, and Bobby Isaac. Ed Stanchak with the Oldsmobile History Center and Art Ponder with DaimlerChrysler Historical Services are due acknowledgment for their assistance in finding the old black and white press photos people still love to see. Anne Cook at the Texas Department of Transportation library has always been unfailingly helpful, and deserves a tip o' the hat for pointing me in the direction of the Texas International Speedway photos.

Thanks are due Jim Whelan, owner of Motion Dynamics in Cedar Park, Texas, for his memories of his days racing in the early Trans-Am series, and for graciously loaning me a photo of his 1966 Trans-Am Mustang. I likewise thank Milt Schornack for sharing his hard-earned opinions about the swiss cheese Super Duty Pontiacs. Others I've interviewed at various times include Gus Scussel, Norm Kraus, Joel Rosen, and Jim Wangers, and those sessions have been continuing sources of useful information.

Much of the information herein was accumulated during my years on staff at the late, great *Super Ford* magazine, but I also relied on other published sources for bits of information. For most of the production numbers and trivia concerning the Hurst cars I relied on *The Hurst Heritage* by Robert Lichty and Terry Boyce. Other noteworthy books I found to be solid sources of information include: *Pontiac Musclecar Performance 1955–1979* by Pete McCarthy, *The Complete Book of Stock-Bodied Drag Racing* by Lyle Kenyon Engel and the editorial staff of *Auto Racing* magazine, *King Richard I: The Autobiography of America's Greatest Auto Racer* with William Neely, *Trans-Am Racing 1966–1985* by Albert Bochroch, and *Chevrolet Big-Block Muscle Cars* by Anthony Young.

I must also thank, with maximum possible gratitude, the car owners who allowed me to photograph their musclecars. They are, in alphabetical order: Dennis Barnes, Elmhurst, Illinois, 1971 Grand Spaulding Demon GSS; Mike Bell, Houston, Texas, 1965 Shelby GT350 Mustang; Paul and Tammie Bilberry, Tuscola, Texas, 1969 Grabber Orange Boss 302 Mustang, 1999 Viper ACR; Curtis Burton, Houston, Texas, 1968 Shelby GT500KR convertible; Kevin Carbaugh, Lancaster, Pennsylvania, 1970 Yenko Deuce; Larry Christensen, Arvada, Colorado, 1967 Camaro Indy pace car, 1969 Yenko SC 427 Camaro, 1969 Camaro Indy pace car, 1997 Brickyard 400 pace car; Tom Daniel, DeSoto, Texas, 1963 1/2 Galaxie Sports Hardtop with 427 SOHC; Glen and Joan Duncan, Katy, Texas, 1971 Pontiac Trans-Am; Gregg Cly, Garland, Texas, 1964 Mustang Indy pace car, 1967 Super Stock "WO 23" Hemi Dodge Coronet, 1968 Camaro Z/28; 1979 Mustang Indy pace car; Ed Giolma, Richardson, Texas, 1961 Royal Pontiac Super Duty race car; Bill Jester, Texas, 1970 Mach 1 Texas International Speedway pace car; Chris Leard, Houston, Texas, 1961 NASCAR

If the 1920s are remembered for the everyman Model T Ford and the 1950s are remembered for tail fins, then plenty of people will remember the musclecar era for the cartoonish graphics, win-at-all-costs rear wings, and gobs and gobs of horsepower.

Ford Starliner; Bill McPeak, De Land, Florida, 1986 Omni GLHS; Jeff Peterson, Ft. Worth, Texas, 1963 "Ramcharger 426" Plymouth Sport Fury; Brian Pulis, Austin, Texas, 1970 Boss 302 Mustang; Kevin Rich, Pflugerville, Texas, 1967 Trans-Am Mustang; Carl Riegger, Allentown, Pennsylvania, 1966 Chevy II L79 sedan; Bill and Rita Schultz, Roseville, Michigan, 1969 Royal Bobcat GTO; Alan Spry, Abilene, Texas, 1970 AAR 'Cuda, 1970 Plymouth Superbird (with extra gratitude for Mike Owens, who graciously allowed us to photograph the cars at his home-built vintage Texaco station); Dave Swisher, Austin, Texas, 1969 Camaro Z28 cross ram.

Next, thanks to the owners through the years who let me drive their special muscle machines. During my time at *Super Ford* magazine I had the good luck to drive everything from small-block Shelby Cobras to 1990s-style Mustang Cobras, so, Tom Wilson, here's some thanks for hiring me. Thanks also to: Stephen Siegel, who trusted me to pilot his 1970 Hemi Charger R/T SE, his 1969 Hemi Daytona, and his Dodge Viper; Tom Daniel, who let me drive his Cammer Galaxie; Gregg Cly, who has let me drive all manner of classic cars from his dealership, including a 1967 Super Stock Coronet, SS396 Nova, 1970 SS396 Camaro, 427 Galaxie, 406 tri-power Galaxie, 1964 GTO, Boss 351 Mustang, and 1968 L78 Chevelle SS. To my cousin David Rigsby, I still remember your 1983 Hurst/Olds Cutlass. Hell, I'll even thank the nameless used car salesman from 20 years ago who tossed me the keys to the 1974 Hurst/Olds for a test drive. There are others, more than I can list here, but all helped give me a well-rounded feel for the machines I'm writing about in this book.

And finally, to my daughter Kelly, this book you're holding in your hands is why Daddy was locked in his office all those nights. Writing it wasn't as fun as playing with you, but at least now we can look at the pretty pictures together. . . .

INTRODUCTION

The Nastier Musclecars

There are musclecars, and then there are *muscle-cars*—pee-your-pants, shred-your-tires, scary, race-ready, uncontrollable *musclecars*. Granted, it's not always easy to make so fine a distinction between what are basically just overpowered, underbraked domestic sedans, but a close examination reveals more than one branch of the super-car family tree.

In the 1960s Detroit produced two breeds of muscle machines. One type was produced in huge numbers for general public consumption. These cars had the look, the advertising push, the image, and the creature comforts. They also had powerful V-8s underhood, some ridiculously powerful, but they were still ultimately designed to be street cars, something the average person could drive to work and back, and maybe have fun with on Saturday night.

Sales of these cars were huge. Cars like the standard Pontiac GTO, the SS396 Chevelle, Nova SS350, and Camaro SS350, the average 383 Plymouth Road Runner and Dodge Super Bee, the Challenger R/T, Ford Torino 390 GT, and on down the long list could be found on every block of middle America.

Then there was the *other* type of musclecar. To find this kind of muscle machine you had to research the fine print on the order form, or be a favored racer, or—at the very least—be well-off financially. These maximum musclecars were usually built strictly for racing, or to qualify as a "production" car so they would be recognized by racing sanctioning bodies. Some seemed to be built purely for the purpose of one-upping a rival automaker. Others were built by independent car dealers and small manufac-

turers to boost sales and help the dealers stand out from the pack.

Examples include the Max Wedge Dodges and Plymouths, the Ford Thunderbolts and Lightweight Galaxies, the Hemi-powered Super Stock Mopars, the NASCAR-inspired Ford Talladegas and Daytona Chargers, and clandestinely built COPO Chevrolets. In modern times the Ford Mustang Cobra R serves as a fine counterpart to yesterday's Shelby Mustangs.

Occasionally the line between the two types of musclecars was blurred. A few of the factory race cars and dealer specials were as easy for the average Joe to purchase as a six-cylinder Falcon. (Or not purchase, as the case may be. As revered as they are now, many a Plymouth Superbird sat forlornly on dealers' lots for years, the cars' towering wings and droopy noses the butt of countless jokes.) Cars like the Trans-Am-inspired Boss 302 Mustang, Dodge T/A Challenger, and Pontiac Trans-Am were sold *en masse* right alongside station wagons and floaty luxury sedans.

Categorizing these cars is no exact science, but in these pages we celebrate the nastier, crankier, race-bred, and race-inspired musclecars. "Maximum muscle" does not refer to your average GTO, Road Runner, or Mach 1—fine cars all, and what most of us could afford—but the legends were started by the cars way out there on the edge of control, like the super stock Hemis, the 427-powered Fords, the Super Duty Pontiacs, the Yenko Camaros, and Mr. Norm's Dodges. Call them hero cars and praise them or, if you're in a contrary frame of mind, call them irresponsible, dangerous, and wasteful, but you can never call them slow, and they were never boring.

Detail, 1970 Plymouth AAR 'Cuda—one of the more striking cars to emerge from factory racing efforts. Subtlety was the first characteristic lost during the 1960s performance wars.

DRAG RACING SPECIALS

Although the first recognizable, organized drag race was flagged in 1948, sanctioned drag racing competition really got its start in the United States in 1951 with the formation of the National Hot Rod Association (NHRA). Prior to that, most straight-line, speed-oriented contests were conducted on dry lake beds in California, or, starting in 1949, the Bonneville salt flats in Utah. In the immediate postwar era, the Southern California Timing Association was the primary sanctioning body for recording new speed records. Home-built hot rods were the order of the day, with drivers lashing them to ever-higher speeds across the high desert sands. Modified hot rods also screamed and burned rubber between stoplights in cities across the country, giving the infant sport of drag racing the most dubious reputation of all motorsports.

Life magazine, in a cover story from April 1957, pointed out the rising conflicts. "As the sport grows, so does the controversy over it," the magazine reported. "Safety groups and some police officers feel that the glorification of speed on the strips infects the teenagers with a fatal spirit of derring-do on the highways. The young drivers are finding the road to respectability a rough one."

Oddly enough, that road to respectability passed through the pages of the fledgling *Hot Rod* magazine. Established in 1948, *Hot Rod* was practically the only national forum for the

The Z-11 Impala was arguably Chevrolet's most potent factory drag car. The Z11 option combined a special 427-ci version of the 409 W-head V-8 with aluminum front sheet metal, for a fantastic power-to-weight ratio. The first batch was built in late 1962, with another run following in January 1963. The Z11 option was a serious commitment—it cost $1,250. *Mike Mueller*

Pontiac's performance image revolved around the Tri-Power induction system. The 1961 389 V-8, shown here in top Tri-Power trim, was rated at 368 horsepower.

of the type of street performance a buyer could expect. Drag racing decided which automaker's cars were hot and which were not.

The battle for supremacy ebbed and flowed. In the early days of drag racing and speed record runs, the first inexpensive, mass-produced V-8, the flathead Ford, ruled the strip. Chopped, fenderless Fords became the prototype hot rod. Oldsmobiles and Cadillacs also became favorites upon the introduction of new overhead-valve V-8s in 1949. But the release of the small-block Chevrolet V-8 in 1955 changed the balance of power for decades. With its compact dimensions, easy parts interchangeability, lightweight casting, and low price, the small-block V-8 earned the loyalty of legions of drag racers. And with the small-block engine in Corvette states of tune, complete with Duntov cam, dual four-barrel carbs, and then fuel injection, racers could piece together a wide variety of combinations.

With the expansion of the Stock Eliminator class in NHRA, and especially the Super Stock class in 1957, there was a home for stock-bodied cars to compete heads-up for bragging rights. Rooted in the 1950s, the Super Stock class proved the perfect battleground for the musclecar fight for supremacy that would take place during the 1960s.

drag racing crowd, and those who argued in favor of the idea that sanctioned competition on legal tracks *discouraged* street racing. If kids had a legal place to race, the reasoning went, they wouldn't be so quick to throw down the gauntlet on main street. As the magazine grew in circulation, so did its influence.

Hot Rod editor Wally Parks backed up the magazine's editorial stance with action, providing the momentum for the creation of the NHRA. With Parks at the helm, the NHRA established rules for competition and safety standards, and created a variety of racing classes. The forum for long-term growth of the sport was set.

As drag racing grew throughout the 1950s, the business community began to take it seriously also. A growing list of entrepreneurs made fortunes selling an ever-expanding list of custom speed parts to eager drivers. And finally, another path to respectability of sorts was worn by the Detroit automakers.

The Big Three slowly discovered drag racing was a useful, if controversial, battleground for establishing which company made the hottest cars. Then, as now, drag racing was the most grassroots-oriented of all motorsports. Show up with a helmet and seatbelts and you can drive the family sedan, or even the family truck, up to the line and cut a time. So to be able to dominate at the dragstrip, heads-up, side-by-side with the competition, in a near-stock auto, was a genuine indicator

GM Power

Intracorporate rivals Chevrolet and Pontiac provided some of the best entertainment at the strip. Both makes carried considerable advantages to the track in the late 1950s. Chevrolet had the quick-revving small-block V-8, and Pontiac was also blessed with stout engines. Both had long rear overhangs, which aided traction, and Chevrolet and Pontiac offered four-speed transmissions at a time when Ford, Chrysler, and Rambler drivers were stuck with three-speeds.

Additionally, in the late 1950s both divisions were headed by people who believed in racing as a means to sell cars. At Chevrolet, chief engineer Ed

The 1961 Super Duty Pontiacs were the last to require car owners to order the engine parts over the counter. This example, raced by Royal Pontiac, ran the 389 V-8; late in 1961 Pontiac released the 421-ci V-8.

Cole was the sparkplug firing the cylinders. Cole pushed aggressively for the installation of fuel injection on the Corvette, along with other performance upgrades. Chevrolet's advertising agency capitalized quickly on the street credibility of its new engine. Print advertising bragged of racing wins racked up in 1955. The 1955 Chevy's new nickname was "the hot one." Victories such as a record-breaking run up Pike's Peak were all fodder for advertising.

Throughout the 1950s the small-block rode a fast-rising escalator of horsepower, starting with 1955's 265-ci Power Pack V-8, which produced 180 horsepower thanks to a four-barrel carburetor and dual exhaust. In 1956 buyers could order a dual four-barrel induction system that boosted horsepower to 225. In 1957 Chevrolet bored out the 265 to 283 cubic inches, which in dual four-barrel trim produced 245 horsepower. The new Rochester fuel injection system bumped power up to 283, giving Chevrolet bragging rights to an engine that churned out one horsepower per cubic inch. With these

weapons, Chevrolet was able to pull ahead of the competition at the dragstrip.

One potential complication in the rush for racing glory was the Automobile Manufacturers Association (AMA) 1957 ban on factory-sponsored racing. This voluntary, industry-wide action was a response to increasingly bad press and threats from Washington about auto safety. However, the "ban" was only a complication if it was followed, and in that regard compliance was spotty. Ford followed the voluntary ban scrupulously, but Chevy and Pontiac treated the gentleman's agreement with a wink and a nod, pouring support out the back door, or sometimes even the front.

A predictable side effect of a budding performance war was a gradual drift to larger engines. Cubic inches are crucial in straight-line performance contests, and Chevy was a leader there, too. The Bow-tie boys introduced a 348-ci "big-block" V-8 for the 1958 model year. The W-head V-8 was physically larger than the existing Chevy V-8 introduced in 1955, with no parts crossover,

The Z11 V-8 was the ultimate expression of the W-head engine family. Based on a stroked 409, the Z11 actually displaced 427 cubic inches and was underrated at 430 horsepower; 500 was closer to reality. The Z11 engine had its own unique intake manifold and heads. *Mike Mueller*

hence the "big-block" designation. (And also the birth of the "small-block" tag for the 265/283 engine family.) The beefier block allowed for larger displacements, allowing Chevrolet to beef up both its car and truck lines.

In four-barrel trim the 348 was rated at 250 horsepower, but race-minded buyers could order the engine with three-two-barrel induction, mechanical cam and lifters, and an 11.0:1 compression ratio, good for 315 horsepower. In between were 348s tuned to 280 and 300 horsepower.

In 1959 the top 348 W-head V-8 produced 335 horsepower, thanks to an increase in compression ratio. In 1961, the 348's final year in Chevy passenger cars, the triple-two-barrel version was good for 350 horsepower.

Powerful as it was, the 348's competitive edge was short-lived. The Dodge 383-ci V-8 was launched in 1959 with a dual-four-barrel option, and Mopar lovers with money could order a 1959 Chrysler with a thumping 413-ci V-8. Ford lagged behind a bit, as their 352-ci V-8 introduced in 1958 did not offer the

high-horsepower levels of other makes, but a 352 Special in 1960 and a much hotter 390-ci V-8 introduced in 1961 kept the pressure on Chevrolet.

Chevrolet's response was a 409-ci version of the W-head big-block. Introduced late in 1961, the engine's extra cubic inches came via both a bore and stroke increase over the 348's dimensions. With a single four-barrel carburetor, it produced 360 horsepower and 409 ft-lbs of torque. Due to the late introduction, few 409 Impalas were built that first year, but the handful that rolled off the line earned big reputations, fast. The Impala, with new SS trim and sloping Sport Coupe roofline, was immediately recognized as just about the hottest thing on the street or strip. Stock street versions cut quarter miles ranging from the high-14s to the mid-15s depending on gearing.

The combination was an instant winner in drag racing competition. In Super Stock competition the 1961 409 Impalas, driven by hotshoes like Don Nicholson and Frank Sanders, were clocking 13.5 and 13.6 quarter-mile times and winning regularly.

In 1962 Pontiac put the whole package together—lightweight body panels, 421 Super Duty engine, and big brakes—and it paid off in a big way at the track. Catalina hardtops like this one were the most popular choice for Super Duty equipment, but the hardware could also be ordered in Catalina sedans and the Grand Prix sport coupe. *Mike Mueller*

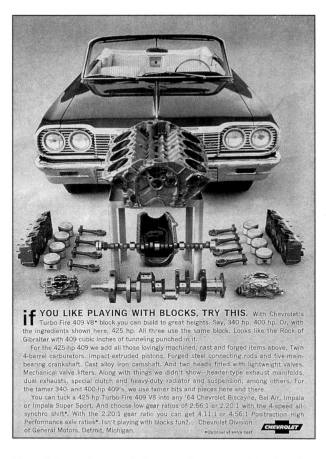

Chevrolet may have ended corporate sponsorship of racing in 1963, but as this ad from 1964 shows, some within the company still knew how to get a point across. Using a "playing with blocks" angle, the ad cleverly lists the engine parts that were obviously intended for racing; "Twin 4-barrel carburetors. Impact-extruded pistons. Forged steel connecting rods and five-main-bearing crankshaft . . . Mechanical valve lifters . . . header-type exhaust manifolds." Listing the available 4.11 and 4.56 axle ratios was another not-so-subtle hint about the 425-horse 409's intended use.

The 409 Impala SS was the dominant car in drag competition that year, with Nicholson capturing such prizes as the Stock Eliminator trophy at the 1961 NHRA Winternationals. Nicholson's 409 was a huge crowd favorite.

The 409 was strengthened further late in the year with an eye on 1962. The most obvious upgrade upon opening a 409 Impala hood was a dual four-barrel option. Just as significant were the redesigned cylinder heads with larger valves. The pistons were also redesigned to provide a larger quench area, the oiling capabilities were improved, and the valvetrain revamped. As *Hot Rod* magazine reported in 1962 "All of Chevy's work on the 409 since its introduction has been aimed toward improving its breathing ability and torque output at high rpm. These efforts have been rewarded by reasonable success." The hottest 409 V-8 was rated at 409 horsepower, and even the single four-barrel

Although usually associated more with road racing, Chevrolet's Corvettes were not an uncommon sight at the drag strip. Until 1963 the Corvette used a solid rear axle, suitable for drag-style launches. The 1962 model pictured here was drag raced heavily in the early 1960s, and was ordered with racing hardware such as oversized, heavy duty brakes, large 15x5.5-inch wheels, positraction rear end, 327-ci V-8 with fuel injection, and "Direct Flow" exhaust.

Although most of those who ordered the 426 Ramcharger V-8 paired the engine with one of the stripped-down body styles such as the Savoy or Belvedere, the powerful wedge could also be ordered in high-end models like the Sport Fury. Sport Fury equipment included special side moldings and trim, bucket seats, a center console, and special upholstery, hub caps, and steering wheel. The 1963 Sport Furys equipped with the 426 carried no external engine identification, although the exhaust note was hard to miss.

version's rating rose to a stout 380, thanks to the above changes and a redesigned intake manifold. In the Super Stock classes, drivers were putting the revised 409s into the high 12s in the quarter mile. In 1963, additional tweaks resulted in the L80 version of the 409 being uprated to 425 horsepower.

Beyond its reputation on the strip and among the greasy fingernail crowd, the 409 carved out a name for itself in mainstream America. Long before the numerals "409" designated a household cleaner, practically every young man in America and more than a few women knew the 409 Chevy was the hot engine to own. The Beach Boys hit song "409," a love sonnet to an engine, must have had Chevrolet execs performing office-corridor cartwheels at their good fortune from this free publicity windfall.

The 409 Impala SS was *the* object of desire among gearheads in 1961 and 1962, but it was still just a street car powered by the hot engine of the moment. What followed in late 1962 and 1963, however, could never be confused with a mere street car. The 1963 Z11 Impala (so named because of the package's option code, RPO Z11) was a genuine factory-built race car. Chevrolet had previously built cars with hot engines suitable for racing, and a few special project Corvettes, but had never gone so far as gutting production cars and tuning the engines to the ragged edge for racing class competition. The Z-11 used weight-saving tactics such as an aluminum front end, with cut out bumper brackets. Unnecessary poundage such as the heater, radio, and insulation was removed. The car was powered by a special stroked version of the 409, with a 12.5:1 compression ratio, special

The 1963 426 Ramcharger V-8 came with either 11.0:1 compression ratio and 415 horsepower, as shown, or 13.5:1 compression and 425 horsepower. The 16-inch "short ram" intake manifold helped move peak performance higher up the rpm band.

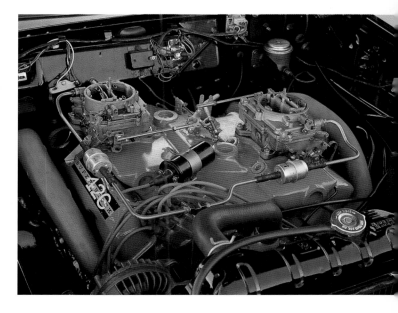

The pushbutton controls for the automatic transmission were a unique feature of the Chrysler corporation. The system was even available with the high-flying 426 Ramcharger V-8. Most racers found the controls easy to use.

heads, and a unique dual four-barrel intake. Displacing 427 cubic inches, the Z11 powerplant was rated at 430 horsepower. The car itself weighed in at roughly 3,350 pounds.

This diligent search for horsepower may have been somewhat counterproductive, however. In 1962 the NHRA, trying to get a handle on the new breed of factory exotic race cars, created the FX (Factory Experimental) classes, which allowed for special low-production engines and more modifications. In 1963 they instituted a 427-ci displacement limit for Super Stocks, as well as a power-to-weight ratio limit. In the NHRA's eyes, the "Super" had taken precedence over the "Stock" part of Super Stock, thanks to cars like the Z-11 Impala, "swiss cheese" lightweight Super Duty Pontiacs, and 413-ci and 426-ci "Max Wedge" Mopars. Many of these cars

were reclassified in the FX classes. The Z-11 was one such factory monster bumped from Super Stock competition in 1963 (although if put together in just the right way, the Z-11 could still compete in some Super Stock classes).

With only 57 examples built, the Z-11s were few in number but made a big impact on the track. "Dyno" Don Nicholson and Ed Shartman raced Z-11 Impalas, and racked up their share of victories. But Dave Strickler, driving his "Old Reliable" Z-11, was especially successful, winning such prizes as the class win at the 1963 NHRA Nationals.

The Z-11 Impalas, in conjunction with the new 427-ci "mystery motors" built for stock car racing (covered in greater detail in chapter 2), proved to be the last great factory race cars from Chevrolet for quite some time. The Z-11 was a victim of corporate suicide—GM's 1963 ban on factory-sponsored racing activity. Despite racing success, an antiperformance mentality had infected upper management at General Motors, resulting in the infamous January 1963 memos that were passed down to all divisions. Unlike the voluntary 1957 AMA "ban" on racing, this time GM was fully committed, with harsh penalties threatened to managers who came to work smelling of factory-sponsored tire smoke.

In truth, 1963 also revealed that Chevrolet was about to be overwhelmed by a concerted factory effort from the Mopar brigades. The Ramcharger Dodges and stripped-down Plymouths with the Max Wedge 426 engine slapped down the competition at the drag strip during most of the year. Still, Chevrolet produced enough hot engine options for their street cars to maintain a respectable presence on the dragstrip throughout the decade. The 396 Chevelle, first introduced in late 1965, and the SS396 Camaro, rolled out for 1967, provided good raw material for racing cars.

Another Chevrolet seemingly built with drag racing in mind was the L79 Chevy II of 1966 and 1967. The L79 327-ci small-block was tuned to 350 horsepower, which provided a fantastic power-to-weight ratio when installed in the compact Chevy II. The engine could be ordered in the most bare-bones, radio- and heater-delete Chevy II imaginable. It was hard to picture any other function for the car but racing, despite official protestation otherwise.

Later in the decade, crafty Chevrolet dealers discovered clandestine methods of ordering Camaros and Chevelles with the company's wild 427-ci Corvette motors. These "COPO" (Central Office Production Order, detailed more in chapter 5) cars represented a whole new round of factory muscle perfectly at home at the dragstrip.

The battle of the factory lightweight musclecars produced many scenes such as this one where Dave Strickler's Z-11 Impala faced off against a Tasca Ford lightweight Galaxie. More often than not, the Chevys won such confrontations. Despite the lightening, the large Galaxies still carried excess weight. Strickler went on to win such prizes as the A/FX title at the 1963 Nationals. *Mike Mueller archives*

Super Duty Pontiacs

In many ways, Pontiac's high-performance arc developed on a parallel course to Chevrolet's. If anything, however, Pontiac was even more aggressive in promoting its racing activities—until, like Chevrolet, the division was cut off at the knees by GM's 1963 racing ban.

The Pontiac braintrust responsible for turning around the Poncho brand's stale image were General Manager Semon E. "Bunkie" Knudsen, Chief Engineer Pete Estes, and the man who would later hold both jobs, John Z. DeLorean. No mere office drones, the trio, especially DeLorean, loved racing and the feel of a hot car, and recognized performance as a way to reach America's youth.

While Chevrolet attacked performance with both small-block and big-block engine families, Pontiac relied on a single overhead valve V-8 design, introduced in 1955, that allowed great flexibility in displacement. Pontiac's attention grabber was a triple-two-barrel induction system called Tri-Power, first introduced in 1957. Although short-lived, Pontiac even built a few fuel-injected 1958 Bonnevilles.

To accommodate racers, Pontiac introduced "Super Duty" engine parts in 1959. Sold over the parts counter, the Super Duty gear included the usual pieces designed to both increase horsepower and keep the engine from blowing apart during the first power shift. The new 389-ci V-8 was the recipient of the stout four-bolt main block, aluminum intake manifold, and header-type exhaust manifolds. Additional improvements, such as performance cylinder heads with larger valves, a high-lift cam design by Pontiac engineer Mac McKellar, and forged high-compression pistons, arrived in 1960. By 1961, the 389-ci V-8 with Super Duty parts was rated at 368 horsepower.

Daytona

Pomona

Phoenix

and you

In Daytona, Richard Petty drove a brilliant blue 1964 Plymouth Super-Stock to victory in the famous Daytona 500-mile race.

At Pomona, Tom Grove's "Melrose Missile" (a 1964 Plymouth Super-Stock) was Top Stock Eliminator in the NHRA Winternationals.

At Phoenix, Dave Strickler and his '64 Dodge Ramcharger won

top honors in the AHRA Dragstrip Championships.

And where do you come in? Perhaps as a spectator to America's latest million-fan sport. (82,240 people watched the gripping action at Daytona, over 50,000 lined the dragstrip at Pomona). To cheer the winning performance of these competition-equipped cars from Chrysler Corporation and to wit-

ness in person the excellence of Chrysler Corporation engineering.

Or, better still, be an active participant in another of America's favorite new pastimes—driving one of the 1964 cars from Chrysler Corporation. The cars that daily demonstrate this same engineering excellence, developed and proved in laboratory and on test-track, and confirmed by competition.

Plymouth • Dodge • Chrysler • Imperial

Chrysler did not shy away from bragging about its racing successes, as this ad from 1964 shows. Beyond the chest-thumping, however, Chrysler tried to make the point that the lessons learned from racing resulted in better passenger cars for the general public.

The Super Duty engines were especially dominating in NASCAR competition, but they also made an impact at the dragstrip, keeping the 409 Chevys from running away with everything. Jim Wangers won Top Stock Eliminator at the 1960 Labor Day NHRA Nationals, giving a Super Duty Pontiac its first NHRA drag racing victory.

Late in 1961, Pontiac released the new 421-ci engine in Super Duty trim, underrated at 373 horsepower. Only a few were built, and they were distributed solely to select racers. But the over-the-counter nature of the Super Duty V-8s was nearing an end. While Pontiac's Super Duty equipment had, to that point, been considered "factory" parts, NHRA rule changes for 1962 required any parts used for racing to actually be sold on production cars—no more back-door, hand-crafted "factory" parts, at least not in Super Stock.

Undeterred, Pontiac bundled the Super Duty engine and suspension parts into an off-the-showroom

package. Although sold to anyone who could bring the cash, Pontiac made no secret of the fact these Catalinas and Grand Prixs were built strictly for racing. As the 1962 Super Duty manual explained: "Super Duty Pontiacs are not intended for highway or general passenger car use and they are not supplied by the Pontiac Motor Division for such purposes."

The 1962 421 Super Duty cars were the strongest assembly-line Pontiacs ever built to that point. The engine was rated at 405 horsepower thanks to an 11.0:1 compression ratio, forged aluminum pistons, an aluminum intake manifold, dual, large-bore four-barrel carburetors with low-restriction air cleaners, header-style exhaust manifolds, and a bypass for the heat riser. The cylinder heads were fitted with undercut and swirl polished 1.92-inch intake valves, and 1.66-inch exhaust valves, plus heavy-duty dual-valve springs and 1.65:1 ratio rocker arms. The cam was a solid lifter McKellar design.

The engine used a race-ready forged-steel crankshaft, a lightweight flywheel, and a block with larger main bearing bores. A six-quart oil pan ensured the parts stayed lubed. A Super Duty single four-barrel 389 V-8 remained in production, rated at 385 horsepower.

Increased horsepower wasn't the only Super Duty strategy. Reducing weight was an obvious tactic as well. Optional lightweight parts included aluminum fenders and inner fenders, an aluminum hood and bumper, and pared-down bumper brackets.

Roger Huntington, reporting for *Motor Trend* in 1962, rode along as adman and racer Jim Wangers cut a 13.9-second quarter mile in a 421 Super Duty Catalina. "Low gear was a rubber-burning fishtail, with the indifferent traction available," he wrote. "A snap shift to 2nd at 5,500 rpm came up in a bit over five seconds. The bellowing open exhausts rattled the whole countryside. Second and 3rd gears almost tore my head off." After his ride, Huntington made a few quick calculations and reported that actual horsepower should be something like 465, given the car's weight and acceleration.

Like Chevrolet, Pontiac's factory drag car program peaked in 1963. Before the GM racing ban took effect, Pontiac produced a special run of extra-lightweight Super Duty cars. These are popularly known as the "swiss cheese" Pontiacs, thanks to the holes drilled in the frame in another weight-saving move. In addition to the existing aluminum sheet metal, the 1963s were fitted with Plexiglass windows. The 421 Super Duty V-8 was strengthened again as well. In top tune, with 13.0:1 compression ratio and cast aluminum header-type exhaust manifolds, the engine was rated at 420 horsepower.

The swiss cheese Catalinas were extremely effective in Super Stock competition, but the weakened frame was a hindrance to those racing in the FX classes, where power levels were much higher. "They had all that aluminum on them, so they didn't have too much weight to carry," recalled Milt Schornack, mechanic and driver at Royal Pontiac in the 1960s and frequent dragstrip competitor. Plus, in Super Stock the cars were limited in tire size and engine modification, so the stress on the frame was not too extreme, he said. But the swiss cheese cars running in B/FX had enough power to mangle the drilled-out frames.

The 1963 Super Duty Pontiacs were the last pure race-bred musclecars from the division. Throughout the rest of the 1960s Pontiac was known for its street musclecars, like the phenomenally popular GTO and the Firebird. The early Super Duty drag cars truly changed Pontiac's image in the eyes of young America. When the GTO hit the scene in 1964, a new generation had learned to believe Pontiacs were fast, and cool.

Olds, Too

Oldsmobile captured imaginations in 1949 with the introduction of its OHV Rocket V-8. Throughout the 1950s Olds developed a reputation as a hot car in the medium-priced market segment thanks to the abilities of the Rocket engine.

By 1957, the Rocket V-8 had sprouted triple-two barrel carburetion. The J2 Rocket engine, at 371 cubic inches, produced 300 horsepower. That figure

The 426-ci Ramcharger wedge V-8 replaced the 413 in 1963. The engine underwent several revisions in a short time span. The Stage II version, introduced later in 1963, switched to higher-flow carburetors, requiring the throttle bore holes in the intake manifold to be enlarged. The hotter Stage III 426 lasted into 1964, but it was soon thereafter replaced by the Hemi. *DaimlerChrysler Corporate Historical Collection*

The inboard headlamps on the Thunderbolt were replaced with air intake hardware. The T-bolt's hood scoop wasn't just for bringing air underhood, it was necessary for clearance with the high-riser 427. The T-bolt shown carries a 427 fitted with experimental hemi cylinder heads, cast in aluminum, and developed by Mickey Thompson. *Mike Mueller*

was upped to 312 horsepower in 1958. But the triple two-barrel induction was dropped for 1959, and with it Oldsmobile's reputation for high performance, at least for a while

Olds sat out the factory-backed dragstrip battles of the late 1950s and early 1960s, focusing its energy on its other reputation, that of an innovator. While Chevy and Pontiac were scratching and clawing each other at the dragstrip, the big news from Olds was the compact Jetfire, which featured a turbocharged, all-aluminum 215-ci V-8. Undoubtedly the most noteworthy Oldsmobile of the 1960s was the Toronado, a full-size, front-wheel-drive coupe powered by a 425-ci V-8.

By the mid-1960s the performance car wave was almost unstoppable, however, with nearly every manufacturer offering *something* track-worthy. Oldsmobile reacted to the 1964 release of the popular Pontiac GTO with its own musclecar, the 442. It lagged behind the competition in sales and performance, but Olds got serious in 1966. That

year they offered what was obviously a drag racing option, the W-30 package. There's no reason to mount a car's battery in the trunk, as the W-30 option did, except to improve weight transfer during drag-style launches.

Checking the W-30 box also shed some of the 442's weight, thanks to fiberglass inner fenders. The 400-ci engine was bolstered by a cold air package featuring huge air intake ducts. Internally, the W-30 was fitted with heavy-duty pistons, a high-lift cam, and a beefed-up valvetrain. Also typical of the time, the W-30 was given a modest power rating of 360, compared to the base 350 horsepower level. Optional triple two-barrel carburetion returned to Oldsmobile order forms as well, if briefly. The 442s so equipped fit comfortably in C/Stock competition.

Chrysler Catches Up

The Chrysler Corporation constructed a formidable performance image in the 1950s thanks to the introduction of the Hemi-head V-8. First installed in

Bill Lawton, driving for Tasca Ford, was one of the successful Thunderbolt drivers. The T-bolts were generally good for mid- to high-11-second elapsed times in 1964—strong, but the Hemi Mopars were usually stronger. Ford built 100 Thunderbolts in 1964. *Mike Mueller archives*

the 1951 Chryslers and labeled the "Firepower" V-8, the Hemi was so named because of the hemispherical shape of the combustion chambers. This cylinder head design allowed superior volumetric efficiency, and impressive power production thanks to large ports and valves and relatively high compression ratios. At least, that's what hot rodders figured out in later years. The first Chrysler Hemi 331-ci V-8s, rated at 180 horsepower and tasked with pulling around the portly 4,000-pound Saratoga models, were not known for blistering performance.

Dodge cars were fitted with the 241-ci versions of the Hemi starting in 1953. But Chrysler Corporation really stepped up its performance image in 1955, with the introduction of the Chrysler C300. Sporting a 331-ci Hemi rated at an unheard-of 300 horsepower, the C300 was the rare combination of luxury and brute power. While certainly powerful enough, the Hemi-powered Chrysler 300 letter series cars had better luck in the stock car racing arena than on the dragstrip. The Chryslers' high price and high tonnage worked against them at the strip, as did the lack of a four-speed transmission—not to

mention unfavorable classification. And who wanted to cut up such a nice interior anyway?

Dodge continued to offer the Hemi in an affordable package, and also moved toward high performance in 1955. That year, Dodge's "Red Ram" Hemi was punched out to 270 cubic inches, and a Super Red Ram version produced 193 horsepower. A D-500 performance package, with even larger displacement and more power, improved Dodge's image in 1956.

In 1959 the first-generation Hemi was replaced by a wedge-head big-block V-8, displacing 413 cubic inches in the big Chryslers, and 383 cubes in the Dodge. These new V-8s carried the Chrysler Corporation to its first real drag racing glory, although not until the early 1960s. Chrysler produced good power straight from the factory, and its experiments with outrageously long, "ram tuned" intake manifolds revealed how much power could be generated for racing.

If 1961 was the year of the 409 Chevy, in 1962 there was no shortage of serious contenders; Dodge and Plymouth certainly came roaring out of the gate. That spring they released a race-tuned 413 V-8 package (named the "Ramcharger" at Dodge, the "Super Stock" V-8 at Plymouth, and commonly known as the Max Wedge) that was clearly built for racing. "The engine is designed for maximum acceleration from a standing start and should be excellently suited for special police pursuit work," Dodge chief engineer George W. Gibson said at the time, leaving no doubt about the engine's expected function.

As introduced, the 413 Max Wedge made its power thanks to an aluminum, one-piece, short-ram intake manifold, tuned to increase power above 4,000 rpm, and two four-barrel carbs fed by a high-capacity fuel pump. The "streamlined" cast iron exhaust manifolds, with 3-inch outlet, were reminiscent of aftermarket headers. A dual-point distributor fired the mix. Out of sight were the forged aluminum pistons designed for an 11.0:1 compression ratio, magnafluxed connecting rods, high-strength valve

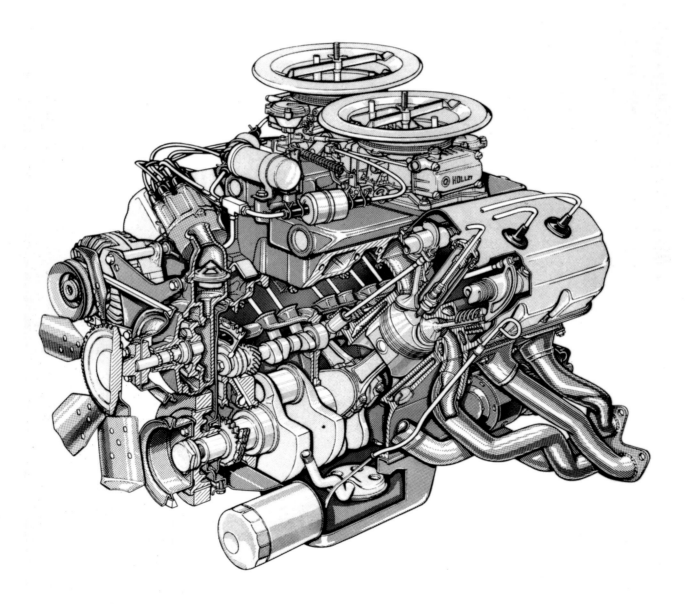

A cutaway of the 1965 426 race Hemi reveals what made the engine such a terror: Large, hemispherical combustion chambers, dual Holley four-barrel carbs on a magnesium cross-ram intake manifold, individual-runner headers, and a double-roller timing chain. The 1965 version of the Hemi was arguably the meanest ever, thanks to the weight reduction provided by the aluminum cylinder heads and magnesium intake. *DaimlerChrysler Corporate Historical Collection*

The team of Ronnie Sox and Buddy Martin campaigned a number of Plymouths during the 1960s, including factory-built specials like the "paper tiger" 1965 lightweight Hemi Belvedere in Super Stock. *DaimlerChrysler Corporate Historical Collection*

spring retainers, and heavy-duty valve springs. A baffled, deep sump oil pan ensured engine parts didn't get sprayed across the track.

The engine showed attention to racing detail with tricks like a smaller crankshaft pulley to limit belt speeds. The Max Wedge 413 was rated at 410 horsepower. An even wilder version, with a 13.5:1 compression ratio, was rated at 420 horsepower. The transmission choices included a heavy-duty three-speed manual with heavy-duty clutch and aluminum clutch housing, or heavy-duty Torqueflite automatic with push-button controls. The push-button automatics, although scoffed at by many racers of the time, did perform well enough to help make up for Chrysler's lack of a four-speed manual.

Helping matters was the fact that 1962 Dodges and Plymouths had been downsized to a mid-size, unibody platform, as the corporation gambled that

buyers were going to turn away from traditional American land yachts in favor of sensible-sized transportation. That proved not to be the case, and Chrysler Corporation sales suffered, but the reduced girth certainly helped from a performance standpoint.

Chrysler applied that lesson further for the 1963 model year. Searching for every advantage in the hyper-competitive market of the early 1960s, Chrysler Corporation made lightweight aluminum body panels available to racers. The company offered paper-thin fenders, hoods, bumper mounting parts, and splash shields, with only minor differences between the Dodge and Plymouth packages. An optional trunk-mounted battery setup helped further with weight transfer. The Max Wedge engine could also be ordered in all-steel B-bodies.

As if that wasn't enough, there was another upgrade underhood. In 1963 the RB (raised block)

In 1965 Ronnie Sox was the first racer to take a stock-bodied, unblown car into the 9s in the quarter mile. His altered wheelbase (AWB) Plymouth ran a 9.98 on April 25 of that year in York, Pennsylvania. The car ran a Hilborn fuel injection system. *DaimlerChrysler Corporate Historical Collection*

big-block was taken out to 426 cubic inches. With 11.0:1 compression, the 426 Max Wedge spit out 415 horsepower. With optional 13.5:1 compression, output rose to 425—a boon to vendors of aviation fuel everywhere. The 426 represented more than just a bore and stroke job, though. The engine featured a new block, a nodular iron crankshaft, enlarged oil pan, and other oiling improvements. The 426 also represented an upper limit, as the NHRA instituted a 427.2 cubic inch limit for Super Stock powerplants in 1963.

At the dragstrip these lightweight, hopped-up Mopars developed a loyal following of their own. A stable of Chrysler engineers formed the "Ramchargers" car club and began running the Ramcharger Dodges in the early 1960s. The red and white, candy-cane striped Dodges proved so popular and effective they were eventually drafted for "factory

team" duty. Their Plymouth counterparts were the "Golden Commandos."

Among the other heroes were Bill "Maverick" Golden, who won the Stock Eliminator title at the 1963 NHRA season opener at Pomona in a Max Wedge Mopar, and Roger Lindamood, whose "Color Me Gone" Max Wedge, and later, Hemi-powered Dodges were stand-outs. Al Eckstrand cut a winning figure in his "Lawman" Max Wedge Dodge 330 sedan. In 1964 Chrysler got serious about "factory teams," by setting up factory-supported drag racers in every region of the country. One team included Bill Flynn, who raced out of New York and became famous for his "Yankee Peddler" Dodges.

Chrysler Corporation continued selling the Max Wedge 426 package in 1964, at least for the first half of the model year. The Max Wedge engines were impressive, but the engine that followed has since come to *own* professional drag racing. The 426 Hemi introduced in 1964 is still in use in today's Top Fuel and Funny Car ranks, and still winning.

Although related to both the early Hemi V-8s of the 1950s and the wedge-head big-blocks, the 426 Hemi was unique in many ways. Known today as the "race Hemi," the 1964 edition (along with the 1965 and some 1968 examples) delivered the same advantages as the original Hemi, while providing more displacement and heavier-duty components—not to mention a far more radical state of tune. The 1964 426 Hemi ran a compression ratio of 12.5:1. Most parts were obviously designed for performance, such as the double-roller timing chain and header-style exhaust manifolds. Cars built for drag racing were topped by dual four-barrel Holley carbs on an aluminum short ram intake. Engines destined for stock car racing ran a single four-barrel carb.

The dual-quad 426 Hemi was rated at 425 horsepower, like the 426 Max Wedge, although true output was somewhere north of 500. On the new Hemi-powered B-body sedans the lightweight parts inventory expanded to include aluminum doors and Lexan windows, although the hardtops were still primarily all-steel.

In 1965 the performance levels of the new Super Stock Mopars rose to almost absurd levels. The Dodge Coronet and Plymouth Belvedere I lightweight drag cars (designated internally as A990) used thin-gauge steel sheet metal so wispy it was practically see-through. The A990 Stockers had numerous features deleted, including the rear seat, armrests, sun visors, heater, and any pretense of streetability. The 1965 426 Hemi was likewise lightened thanks to aluminum cylinder heads and a magnesium intake manifold.

When Mopar drivers began combining nitromethane fuel and Hilborn injection with the lightweight AWB Dodges, elapsed times dropped into the 8s. The Ramchargers' Jim Thornton was the first, cutting an 8.91 on August 7, 1965. *DaimlerChrysler Corporate Historical Collection*

By the time 1965 rolled around, however, the Super Stock drag racing classes had long since been knocked off the top of the mountain. The FX, or Factory Experimental classes, were the new showcase for the manufacturers' best efforts (FX eventually evolved into today's Funny Car class). Factory Experimental allowed more modifications than Super Stock, and competitors could run any engine their car's manufacturer produced, as long it was of the same year model. Depending on power-to-weight ratios the cars were placed in A/FX, B/FX, or C/FX.

Chrysler put forward a stupendous effort with a small run of altered wheelbase (AWB) Coronets and Plymouths for A/FX in 1965. By moving the front wheels forward 10 inches and rear axles up 15 inches, more of the cars' weight was shifted to the rear, improving traction during launch. These oddly proportioned Mopars utilized the same weight-saving techniques as the super stock editions, plus the hot Hemi.

The NHRA, however, balked at letting the altereds into the show, so the AWB Mopars debuted at the rival American Hot Rod Association (AHRA) Winternationals in Arizona, to great success. Bud Faubel won the Mr. Stock Eliminator title, and the Ramchargers took home Top Stock Eliminator. Both were running ETs in the 10.9-second range. Dick Landy and Bill Flynn were other successful AWB pilots. Ramcharger driver Jim Thornton drove a nitro-burning AWB Dodge to the first 8-second elapsed time by an unblown, stock-bodied automobile.

Although factory created (more or less—most were built at Automotive Conversions, a manufacturer of ambulances and limos and such) the altered wheelbase cars were obviously not something the average car buyer could purchase. However, average Joes were starting to find ways to order the 426 Hemi in 1965, although without factory warranties. Even so, the Hemi was not yet what the sanctioning bodies were willing to bless as a "production" engine. In fact, the 426 Hemi was banned from NASCAR competition in 1965.

And so, after two years as primarily a racing engine option, Chrysler offered the 426 Hemi as a "street" engine starting in 1966. Yes, the 1964 and

A formidable engine at the strip, Ford's 427 SOHC V-8 was never offered in a production car. The chain-driven overhead cam powerplant was sold over the counter, finding a home in dragstrip-bound Galaxies and Mustangs. In action, the 427 "Cammer" was quick-revving, feeling more like a small-block than a bottom-heavy big-block, and put forth a distinctive sound thanks to the engine's several feet of timing chains.

Bill Lawton, in a Tasca Ford 427 SOHC Mustang, squares off against "Dyno" Don Nicholson in an A/FX Mercury Comet. Both were very successful in 1965, with the cars good for 10.9-second quarter miles. Lawton won the NHRA Winternationals Factory Stock Eliminator title. Later in the year, Cammer Mustang drivers switched to an altered wheelbase and fuel injection to keep up with the Mopars. *Mike Mueller archives*

1965 426 Hemi were technically factory production engines, but they were also obviously racing specials built for the sole purpose of beating in Ford's and Chevy's brains. They were hardly streetable engines easily available to the general public—the idea that was the very backbone of the Super Stock drag racing classes and stock car racing in general.

The dramatic new fastback Dodge Charger, along with the Coronet, Plymouth Belvedere, and Plymouth Satellite, were the lucky recipients of the street Hemi in 1966. The street Hemi differed from earlier versions by running dual Carter four-barrel carbs mounted on an inline manifold, a 10.25:1 compression ratio, and milder camming. Of course, "street engine" is a relative term, as the 426 Hemi could not be ordered with common comforts such as air conditioning, but at least the pretense could be maintained.

Almost unnoticed in that year of the Hemi was a smaller, but still potent, factory-tuned drag car, the so-called "D/Dart." The D/Dart, with its 273-ci small-block V-8, was aimed at D/Stock competition.

Dodge sent the little warriors into battle with Holley four-barrel carburetors on modified intake manifolds, a hotter, solid-lifter cam, headers, and a quick-advance distributor. The D/Darts were rated at 275 horsepower, 40 above the standard 273. Few were built.

Beyond the D/Dart, Chrysler decided against production of any factory lightweight super stockers in 1966, but the race cars returned in 1967. That year Chrysler built a small run of super stock Dodge Coronets (coded WO23) and Plymouth Belvedere IIs (coded RO23). Unlike earlier super stockers, these cars were fitted with a modified version of the street Hemi, inline four-barrels, and lower compression ratios. Also, they did not use lightweight body panels, with the exception of a functional thin-gauge steel hood scoop.

With steel sheet metal and a more tractable Hemi, the 1967 super stockers were often purchased with street racing in mind. The base retail price for a WO23 Coronet was $3,875—high compared to the average Coronet, but within the budgets of many lead-footed stoplight warriors.

The last great factory super stock drag cars from Chrysler arrived in 1968. They were perhaps even the greatest, since they teamed the corporation's monster motor, the Hemi, with its smallest cars, the Dodge Dart and Plymouth Barracuda. The Hemi Darts and Barracudas were built in early 1968 by Hurst Performance Research, a company increasingly adept at building limited runs of special cars. As with the earlier lightweights, Hurst put the race cars on a diet. The Dart and Barracuda used fiberglass fenders and hood, acid-dipped doors, and light Chemcor side glass.

The 1968 super stock Darts and Barracudas were built with the race version of the Hemi used earlier in the decade. The engine ran a 12.5:1 compression ratio and Holley four-barrel carburetors perched atop an aluminum cross ram intake manifold. Of the racers who ran the 1968 Hemis, Ronnie Sox and Buddy Martin were likely the best known and most successful. The Sox & Martin Barracuda has earned a spot as an instantly recognizable icon among Mopar enthusiasts.

Ford—Late, But Great

It was a rough time for Blue Oval believers. In 1961 the 409 Chevy cleaned house. In 1962 the 409 was still hot stuff, and so was the 421 Pontiac and 413 Mopar. In 1963 the 426-ci "Max Wedge" Mopars were the new rulers of the strip.

When Ford did finally catch up, however, the company did so in grand style. Ford had let an enviable reputation for performance languish during the late 1950s. The company that was once the backbone of the hot-rodding hobby thanks to the flathead V-8, and even offered supercharged Thunderbirds to the public in the mid-1950s, took the AMA's 1957 ban of factory-sponsored racing quite seriously. Ford division general manager Robert McNamara was especially firm in his belief that cars should be sensible transportation.

"He [McNamara] was a good businessman, but he had the mentality of a consumerist," recalled a

Oldsmobile wasn't a major player in the Super Stock and A/FX wars of the 1960s, but even it couldn't ignore drag racing forever, not if it wanted to attract young buyers with bulging wallets to its showrooms. The 1966 W-30 442 was built with the quarter mile in mind. The W-30 option provided a specially tuned 400-ci V-8, modest weight savings, and a trunk-mounted battery for better weight distribution. The cars were successful in C/Stock events. *Mike Mueller*

Chevrolet may have been officially out of factory-sponsored racing after 1963, but that didn't stop the company from building cars that were race-ready. By offering their hottest engines, like the 350-horsepower L79 327 V-8, in stripped-down sedans like this 1966 Chevy II sedan, Chevrolet provided drag racers with plenty of raw material.

In keeping with its racing mission, the Olds W-30 V-8 used large ducting to feed cold outside air to the engine. The W-30 V-8 was also upgraded with a high-lift camshaft and heavy-duty valvetrain. *Mike Mueller*

later president of Ford, Lee Iacocca, in his 1984 book, *Iacocca, An Autobiography*. "He believed strongly in the idea of a utilitarian car, a car whose purpose was simply to meet people's basic needs. He looked upon most luxury models and options as frivolous and accepted them only because of the higher margins they commanded." McNamara's ideal car, and the legacy of his Ford days, was the Falcon, a car so far removed from high-performance that it's hard to even imagine one on a race track.

When McNamara left the company to become president Kennedy's secretary of defense, Iacocca became Ford division general manager, and he had no problem with high performance. His ideal car, and legacy, was the Mustang.

But the late start left Ford at a disadvantage. Like Chrysler, Ford was hobbled by the lack of a four-speed transmission, which didn't arrive until 1961. The cars were heavy. And Ford's V-8s always seemed to lag just a bit behind in the horsepower department.

Ford's overhead valve FE-series big-block V-8 was introduced in 1958 at 332 and 352 cubic inches. Although a police interceptor version was available, rated at 300 horsepower, it wasn't known to be a terror at the dragstrip. The first sign of life came in 1960, when Ford released a high-performance engine known as the 352 Special, or 352 Interceptor. The Special was a genuine performance engine in that it ran a solid lifter cam, dual-point distributor, individual-runner exhaust manifolds, high compression, and a small Holley four-barrel carburetor on a light aluminum intake manifold. It was rated, perhaps optimistically, at 360 horsepower.

From there, development of a race-ready FE engine proceeded quickly, with varying success. The 352 was enlarged to 390 cubic inches in 1961, with the top engine producing 375 horsepower. Ford then crossed the one horsepower-per-cubic-inch threshold again with a triple-two-barrel induction system that raised power to 401. As rivals hurried out their own big-inch engines, Ford enlarged the 390 to 406 cubic inches in 1962, although the 390 was still available. With the trio of two-throat carbs, the 406 was rated at 405 horsepower.

At the dragstrip, results were mixed for the high-performance Galaxies. During the 1961 NHRA Winternationals Les Ritchey cut a hot 13.33 at 105 miles per hour in a 401-horse 390, raising a few eyebrows, but the 409 Chevys were still the cars to beat. Ford tried harder in 1962. The company commissioned Dearborn Steel Tubing to built a short run of 11 lightweight 406 Galaxies for A/FX competition. For the lightweight Galaxies, Ford relied primarily on

The first 426 Hemi identification in 1966 was a modest emblem. By 1971 billboard-sized graphics screamed the engine's name.

fiberglass hoods, fenders, and decklids to reduce weight rather than the aluminum panels employed by GM and Chrysler.

Still, the Fords came in on the heavy side. Plus, whereas some manufacturers underrated their performance engines, some of the Ford big-blocks had rather optimistic horsepower ratings. The new Ramcharger Dodges and Golden Commando Plymouths, with their smaller dimensions and unibody frames, not to mention larger engines, were the biggest obstacle to overcome.

The 427 engine, introduced in 1963, was the key to Ford's ascendance in drag racing, as well as most other forms of motorsport. Like the Chrysler 426 Hemi and later 427 Chevy V-8, the engine's displacement was determined by the 7-liter limit NHRA and NASCAR sanctioning bodies allowed. Unlike earlier Ford FE big-blocks, however, the 427 was designed from the beginning to be a racing engine first, rather than a hopped-up passenger car motor.

The 1963 427 engine was released with an extremely rigid block, and featured cross-bolted main bearing caps for optimum bearing alignment. The pistons were impact-extruded, the connecting rods reinforced. The exhaust valves were made of forged steel with chrome stems. Solid valve lifters worked with a high-lift cam. Modern touches included an optional transistorized ignition and an alternator charging system, rather than the generators still commonly in use. Exhaust manifolds were header-style, with individual runners. The 427 came with an aluminum intake manifold, with either single four-barrel or dual four-barrel induction. In dual-carb trim, Ford rated the

The Super Stock Dodges for 1967 were easily identified by their large, functional steel hoodscoops. Although items like the heater, radio, and windshield wiper motor and assembly were deleted to save weight, the 1967 Super Stocks were not "lightweights" in the traditional sense. They used no aluminum or fiberglass body parts. Dodge built 55 Super Stock Coronets in 1967. All were painted white, with black vinyl interior.

427 at 425 horsepower. With single four-barrel it was rated at 410.

Armed with the new engine, and an aerodynamic, mid-year semi-fastback hardtop body style, Ford again tried to make inroads against the dominant Mopars. Their newest effort was another run of lightweight Galaxies. Once again employing fiber-

glass fenders and hood, Ford eliminated weight wherever possible. The cars were shipped without heaters, trunk mats, spare tires, or even much sound deadener. The bumpers and brackets were aluminum. The Galaxies even looked utilitarian, as they were only available with white paint and red interiors. Exact numbers are fuzzy, but approximately

The 1967 Super Stock Dodge Coronets and Plymouth Belvederes used a modified version of the 10.25:1 compression "street" Hemi, rather than the super-high-compression race Hemis of earlier years. Modifications were made primarily to the intake manifold and carburetors, which improved fuel flow.

200 of the lightweight 1963 Galaxies were built. Ford followed up with a run of 50 1964 lightweight Galaxies. The 1964 models' new bodystyle was beefed up with a unique "teardrop" blister hood scoop that vented the engine compartment, as well as opening up room for the taller "high riser" version of the 427 engine.

Still, the Galaxies were roughly 150 to 200 pounds heavier than the competition, with elapsed time usually in the low 12-second range. Victories were few. After spotty results with the gutted Galaxies, in 1964 Ford deployed its version of the tactical

nuke. This time, they dropped the powerful but heavy 427 into the intermediate-size Fairlane, and lightened the car further with fiberglass body parts, down to about 3,225 pounds. The result was the 427 "Thunderbolt," arguably the most memorable of Ford's factory drag cars.

Ford followed the rules for Super Stock competition to the letter, giving the Thunderbolts favorable classification. The Thunderbolts were generally good for 11.80 elapsed times that year, good enough to bring home the trophies. Gas Ronda won the 1964 NHRA World Stock Eliminator title in a Thunderbolt, largely by racking up points racing coast-to-coast in several NHRA regional points meets. Phil Bonner likewise won the AHRA Mr. Stock Eliminator title in a Thunderbolt. The initial run of 11 Thunderbolts went to established drag racers like Ronda, Bonner, Dick Brannen, and Mickey Thompson, but Ford built two more batches, eventually bringing production to a round 100 cars.

The next step in Ford's "Total Performance" campaign was an indication of how far the company was prepared to go to win. Chrysler's Hemi was the engine to beat in the mid-1960s. Without the ability to go above seven liters of displacement thanks to the racing rule book, and most of the easy hot-rodding development already behind them, Ford had to turn to increasingly exotic designs to one-up Mopar.

The result was the overhead cam 427, an engine developed in a remarkably short time thanks to the success of the 426 Hemi. Based on the FE block design but crowned by cylinder heads that housed one camshaft per bank, plus hemispherical combustion

Super Stock Dodges and Plymouths were sold with trunk-mounted batteries, which improved weight distribution to the rear during drag-style launches. The cars used huge, powerful Super Stock batteries to deliver maximum cranking power.

chambers, the 427 SOHC was an imposing sight. The cams were spun by roughly six feet of timing chain, which was hidden behind a massive front cover. With a single four-barrel carburetor, the SOHC 427 produced just shy of 600 horsepower.

The sanctioning bodies, however, took an increasingly dim view of the exotic powerplants. NASCAR disallowed the SOHC 427 altogether, leaving it suitable solely for drag racing, usually in A/FX or, later, Funny Car competition. Unlike the pushrod FE 427, the "Cammer" 427, as it became known, was never installed in a production automobile. It was only sold over the counter, and usually only to well-funded race teams.

That is, with one important exception—although an exception that could never be called a production car. If the various Galaxies were disappointing at the strip, by 1965 they were old news anyway. The new face of Ford was the shockingly popular Mustang. Ford was on its way toward building more than 681,000 in the extended 1965 model run. Teaming the Mustang with the radical 427 SOHC was a natural move for A/FX competition.

Ford assigned race shop Holman-Moody of Charlotte, North Carolina, to build 11 427 SOHC Mustangs (one of which was for show, the others to race) for A/FX competition. The operation involved more than just dropping a big motor into a Mustang, however. As was legal in A/FX, the rear wheels were moved three inches forward for better weight distribution. Unique traction bars were welded into place as part of the drag-style rear suspension. Holman-Moody cut out the front shock towers, and replaced the stock suspension with a custom leaf-spring design. This made room for the massive Cammer V-8, although just barely. The headers had to be custom made, no small task given the tight confines of the engine compartment. Naturally, the entire front-end bodywork was fiberglass, as were the doors, and the windows were Plexiglas.

The SOHC Mustangs were good for high 10-second ETs initially, with racers like Les Ritchey and Gas Ronda whittling the times down into the 10.6 range. Bill Lawton was especially effective in a Cammer Mustang sponsored by Tasca Ford, notching a big win at the NHRA Winternationals.

Meanwhile, over at Ford's sister division, Mercury, enthusiastic engineers ran a parallel program to the Thunderbolt. Mercury created a run of fiberglass-draped Comets fitted with 427-ci big-block V-8s for A/FX duty. Many Chevrolet drivers were lured over by the promise of the Mercs (not to mention the demise of the Z-11 Impala). They made a huge splash early in the 1964 racing season, before the Chrysler 426 Hemi was ready. Ronnie Sox took the big prize, the FX Eliminator title at the NHRA Winternationals. A B/FX program allowed racers to order special 289-powered lightweight Comets direct through the dealer. These were modified at Bill Stroppe's California facility.

One of Ford's last great super stock projects of the 1960s helped introduce yet another version of the FE big-block engine to the public. Ford had developed an unwanted reputation for winning big in NASCAR, at LeMans, at Indy, in Trans-Am, and to a lesser extent in drag racing, but not translating that performance into a hot street car. The 427 Galaxie, although certainly fast, was always held back by its weight. Ford dropped the 427 big-block in the mid-size Fairlane, but the car was packaged so anonymously it went mostly unnoticed. And frankly, the Mustang 390 GT just couldn't keep up with hot Chevys, Pontiacs, and Mopars on the street.

Performance-minded dealer Tasca Ford of Providence, Rhode Island, dropped a modified 428 police interceptor engine in the Mustang creating a 13-second street car in the process. With the viability of the concept proven, plus an editorial assist by *Hot Rod* magazine, Ford planned a 428 "Cobra Jet" option for the Mustang for midyear release. Naturally, a special run of Super Stock Cobra Jet Mustangs helped get the news out to the right crowd.

The 50 Super Stock Cobra Jet Mustangs Ford built were lightened, although not through fiberglass or aluminum body panels. Their weight was trimmed through the deletion of sound deadener, undercoating, heater, and radio. They were fitted with drum brakes, rather than the heavier discs. The battery was mounted in the trunk, by then a familiar drag racing modification. The Super Stock Cobra Jets debuted at the 1968 Winternationals, where Al Joniec won the Super Stock title. More importantly, however, the 428 Cobra Jet proved to be an engine that could get the job done on the street. Straight off the showroom floor it

The 428 Cobra Jet engine made its debut at the 1968 NHRA Winternationals. Although fine on the race track, the 428 CJ was more important for its contribution to Ford's reputation on the street. Powerful and tractable, the 428 CJ was the street muscle engine Ford had been missing.

Chrysler was up front about the intended use of its super stock Hemis, going so far as placing stickers underhood reminding owners that the cars carried no warranty. Not everyone was deterred—the tag pictured was affixed to a Dodge that was extensively street raced.

The 1968 Super Stock Plymouth Barracudas and Hemi Darts were the last great factory drag cars from Chrysler. The combination of compact A-body and race Hemi helped Ronnie Sox win the AHRA Driver of the Year title in 1968. Sox and Martin's famous Barracuda, campaigned in 1968 and 1969, was nicknamed the "'Lil Boss." *DaimlerChrysler Corporate Historical Collection*

was a legitimate 13-second threat, and Ford partisans no longer needed to feign inattention when a big-block Mopar rumbled up alongside at a stoplight. For once, the promise of the racing version was realized in a legitimately competitive street musclecar.

After the 1968 Cobra Jets, Ford backed out of the factory-built drag car business, but did continue to offer track-oriented options. The various 428 and 429-powered Mustangs and Torinos could be ordered with an optional "Drag Pack" that included an oil cooler, racing-oriented rear end gears, etc. By the early 1970s even these options were gone, requiring Ford drag racers to do the hard work themselves.

AMC Impact

For most of the 1960s, American Motors treated racing as if it were a social pathology. Not surprisingly, that schoolmarmish attitude didn't win over many young buyers.

That changed after the company introduced the Javelin and AMX in 1968. With the two-seat AMX

especially, AMC pushed an aggressive performance image. They bank-rolled land speed racer Craig Breedlove in an effort to chisel the AMX's name in the record books. He succeeded.

In his autobiography *Spirit of America, Winning the World's Land Speed Record* (with Bill Neely), Breedlove remembered, "I had six weeks in which to prepare the car. The runs had to be made in that period because the AMX had not yet been introduced to the public, and American Motors needed the record runs to pump up the advertising campaigns.

"Getting the cars ready meant reworking the suspension and steering systems, so they would handle well at extra-high speeds. I also had to take the engines completely apart and rebuild them. I had to balance all the parts and make sure everything was perfect inside. And it all had to be done with stock parts, because there certainly weren't any speed parts for the AMX," he wrote.

During runs at Goodyear's proving ground in San Angelo, Texas, Breedlove and his wife broke

A Rambler that does the quarter mile in 14.3.

American Motors and Hurst have collaborated on the custom-built SC/Rambler.

It's a limited production car; only 500 units are planned at this time.

Enough to qualify the SC/Rambler for stock classes in drag racing.

The price is $2,998! Which is very little money when you see what it buys.

1. 390 cubic inch AMX V-8 Engine.
2. 4-speed all-synchromesh close-ratio transmission.
3. Special Hurst 4-speed shift linkage with T-handle.
4. A Sun tach mounted on the steering column.
5. Dual Exhaust system with special-tone mufflers and chrome extensions.
6. Functional Hood Scoop for cold-air induction.
7. Twin-Grip differential.
8. 10½" diameter clutch.
9. 3.54:1 axle ratio.
10. Power disc brakes (front).
11. Rear axle torque links.
12. Handling package (heavy-duty front sway bar plus heavy-duty springs and shocks).
13. Heavy-duty cooling system (heavy-duty radiator,

power-flex fan and fan shroud).
14. A 20:1 manual steering ratio.
15. Special application of new Red, White and Blue exterior colors.
16. Two hood Tie-Downs with locking safety pins and cables.
17. Custom Tear-Drop racing mirrors (one each side).
18. Custom Grille.
19. Custom SC/Rambler-Hurst emblem on front fenders/rear panel.
20. Mag styled wheels, 14" x 6", painted specially to complement exterior color scheme.
21. Five E 70 x 14 Goodyear Polyglas™ Wide-Tread tires.
22. Sports steering wheel.
23. Custom-upholstered head restraints in Red, White and Blue vinyl.
24. All-vinyl charcoal seat upholstery with full carpeting.
25. Individually adjustable reclining seats.

There's more, but you get the idea. With this car you could make life miserable for any GTO, Roadrunner, Cobra Jet or Mach 1.

American Motors'/Hurst SC/Rambler

1. Manufacturer's suggested retail price includes all items listed and federal taxes. State and local taxes, if any, and destination charges excluded.

Just in case anyone was too dense to figure out the SC/Rambler's mission in life, AMC thoughtfully provided quarter-mile elapsed times. Although a latecomer to the performance market, AMC made up for lost time with aggressive advertising. AMC and Hurst combined to create 1,512 of the red, white, and blue pocket rockets. The SC/Ramblers built during the later half of the production run were painted with a slightly less flamboyant scheme.

106 national and international speed records. He averaged 175 miles per hour with the 390-ci AMX, and 160 miles per hour with the 290-ci V-8.

For 1969 AMC concentrated on a dragstrip image. The company worked with Hurst Performance Research to create a series of Super Stock AMXs. The SS AMX ran a 390-ci V-8 fed by two Holley four barrels on an Edelbrock intake manifold. The engine ran a 12.3:1 compression ratio, thanks to heads

modified by Crane Cams. Exhaust highlights included a set of Doug's headers. The AMXs were sold with four-speed transmissions with Lakewood bellhousings, and were given specially modified rear suspensions for drag racing. Unnecessary items were deleted to cut weight. Perhaps the best-known of these AMXs was raced by Shirley Shahan, of "Drag-on Lady" fame.

Complementing the AMX was a run of special Ramblers, also massaged by Hurst. Designed with both street performance and F/Stock drag competition in mind, the 1969 Hurst SC/Rambler was likely the most outrageous musclecar to emerge from AMC. An almost comically large hood scoop dominated the exterior, along with a red, white, and blue paint scheme that looked as if it belonged on a funny car.

The SC/Rambler was conceived as a stripped-down musclecar, in Road Runner fashion. The base price was a low $2,998. The money went into the hardware, with standard equipment including a 390 V-8 rated at 315 horsepower, a four-speed transmission with, naturally, a Hurst shifter. The SC/Rambler even came with a Sun tachometer mounted on the steering column, just as could be found on countless Saturday night cruisers across the country. The car was advertised as being able to run a quarter mile in 14.3 seconds. Although the SC/Rambler left behind no great racing heritage, it was a direct by-product of the popularity and influence of drag racing. And though only 1,512 were built it is arguably the single most memorable Rambler, showing what racing ties can do for a car's legacy.

The Detroit automakers abandoned most factory-sponsored drag racing efforts in the early 1970s, and the drag racing-inspired street cars with them. Vast engineering resources were required to meet the new emissions and safety regulations introduced that decade, and the musclecar market had shrunk anyway. But it's doubtful any sport influenced 1960s-era Detroit more than drag racing, and there's still enough evidence prowling around America's dragstrips and cruise nights to prove it.

STOCK CAR SPECIALS

Not surprisingly, the factory-sponsored efforts to create the ultimate stock car package mirrored what was happening on the drag racing side of the track. The Big Three committed an enormous amount of engineering and financial resources in pursuit of the exotic engines and slippery sheet metal that would give them the leg up in NASCAR and USAC (United States Auto Club) stock car competition. Just as quarter-mile competition bred a generation of specialized straight-line muscle-cars for the street, the battles on the superspeedways also resulted in the creation of some very distinct, purpose-built take-home musclecars.

The 1960s saw further deviations from the traditional "stock car" definition. The differences between the cars that raced around Daytona in 1960 and those that burned up the track in 1970 were substantial. The engines, for example, were further removed from "production" status. Yes, technically a Boss 429 was a production engine, but try ordering one for your Torino. Where once racers bought their cars right off dealers lots, by the time the 1960s closed most teams received bare-bones "bodies in white" from the manufacturers. And the nose of dad's family sedan didn't quite scrape the pavement like Richard Petty's Plymouths.

It was a very competitive decade, with bragging rights and a crack at the youth market's collective wallet up for

The Cyclone Spoiler II's most prominent wind-cheating feature was its extended nose with flush grille and headlamps, which replaced the recessed grille of the regular Cyclone. Mercury modified the car's rear bumper for use on the front. The Cale Yarborough edition was marked by red and white colors. *Mike Mueller*

The most aerodynamic choice for racing in Ford's 1961 line-up was the Starliner model. Holman-Moody was the leading source of Ford performance parts and tuning, and the shop prepped many a car for NASCAR, including the one shown here. Owned when new by veteran racer Tubby Gonzales, the car is best remembered as the one Fred Lorenzen drove to a fourth-place finish at Daytona in 1961, after buying the ride from Gonzales.

grabs. Although Chevrolet made a respectable showing of itself in NASCAR in 1961 and 1962, Pontiac was really the dominant make during those years. After GM's 1963 racing ban, however, Ford, Plymouth, and Dodge were the kings of the high banks.

In drag racing, engine torque, weight transfer, and overall vehicle weight were paramount to success. In stock car racing, engine durability and aerodynamics were the keys to winning. Consequently, the focus of stock car engineering during the 1960s could be summed up in two words—engines and aerodynamics. Huge gains were made in both areas, but that didn't necessarily result in superior street cars.

Big Engines

Pontiac blasted out of the 1950s in a cloud of tire smoke, laying a serious holeshot on every other

Detroit automaker, to borrow a little drag racing terminology. The reason was simple: GM's rapidly reviving division basically ignored the 1957 AMA ban on auto racing. Pontiac general manager Bunkie Knudsen was convinced racing success would capture the youth market, and he set up Pontiac's own in-house "Super Duty" group for the purpose of building racing parts.

Starting with a trickle in the late 1950s and swelling to a torrent of parts by 1960, Pontiac began producing forged connecting rods, reinforced blocks, big-valve cylinder heads, aluminum intake manifolds, and solid-lifter cams. These parts gave Pontiac racers an enormous advantage at the beginning of the decade over, for example, Ford racers, who were still sorting out the FE big-block engine family.

Pontiac street and drag racing V-8s of the 1960s earned their performance reputations through the

Tri-Power carburetion setup, but a single four-barrel was required in NASCAR and USAC stock car competition. That was no impediment. The 1961 389-ci four-barrel Super Duty engine was rated at 368 horsepower, the same as the Tri-Power, although in truth the horsepower ratings were whatever Pontiac needed them to be.

The 1960 and 1961 Super Duty V-8s were over-the-counter parts packages, not a production-line engine—a fact that eventually got Pontiac in trouble with the NASCAR rule book, which required any engine raced to be available to the general public. Consequently, in 1962 Pontiac released a 421 Super Duty engine available for order in Catalinas and Grand Prix models.

The 1962 421 Super Duty was the most capable Pontiac V-8 yet, winning big at both the dragstrip and stock car ovals. Behind the talents of Pontiac stock car drivers such as Fireball Roberts, Smokey Yunick, and Marvin Panch, Pontiac progressed from one Grand National (now Winston Cup) win in 1959,

to 7 wins in 1960, 30 wins in 1961, and 22 in 1962. Pontiac won the NASCAR Manufacturers Championship in 1961 and 1962, a feat it hasn't managed to duplicate in nearly four decades.

Although Chevrolet's 409 had earned a reputation as a terror on the dragstrip—it was *the* engine to beat in 1961—it had some shortcomings for stock car racing. The W-head big-block made a decent street performance engine, but it had limited breathing abilities, and a combustion-chamber-in-the-block design that was behind the times. Still, Chevys managed to win 11 Grand National races in 1961 and 14 in 1962, second only to Pontiac's total.

Chevrolet's response to the situation didn't do much for the division's stock car fortunes in the short term, but had a huge effect on the type of street engines enthusiasts could purchase later in the decade.

Chevrolet's replacement for the 409 was the "Mark II" big-block V-8, engineered largely by Dick

Ford's 390-ci FE big-block arrived in 1961. The performance version made its claimed 375 horsepower thanks to a combination of features: the special cylinder heads and solid lifter cam used on the previous year's 352 Special, a 10.6:1 compression ratio, a dual-point distributor, a four-barrel carburetor on an aluminum intake manifold, and header-style exhaust manifolds. Common Holman-Moody modifications included an oil cooler and super tuning. The 390 was powerful but usually outrun that year by the 389 Super Duty Pontiacs.

Keinath. Although conventional in design, the Mark II was definitely modernized and developed with racing in mind. The combustion chamber was moved to the cylinder head, bringing it in line with other contemporary overhead valve designs. The Mark II had performance-shaped ports, splayed valves, a lightweight valvetrain, header-style exhaust manifolds and a high-rise, dual-plane aluminum intake manifold. Its displacement came in at 427 cubic inches, not coincidentally the new maximum allowed by NASCAR.

The infamous Mark II was nicknamed the "mystery motor" by the press in 1963, so called because the security barriers Chevrolet drivers erected around the garages at Daytona prevented anyone from getting a look at the new engines. But everyone knew something was up when Chevrolets easily won the two qualifying races at Daytona, creating a furor in the pits. Junior Johnson, in his Holly Farms Poultry-sponsored Chevrolet, was particularly fast, breaking the record for the qualifying race. The 409 had never been *that* dominating, and Ford Motor Company especially wanted a look at this new "production" engine. Chevrolet's stance was that the Mark II was an upcoming production engine, which was technically true, but certainly nobody could purchase one in 1963.

Chevrolet was allowed to compete with the engine at Daytona, but only after two were sold to Ford to prove they were available for sale. After all the angst generated by Chevy's new motor, though, it

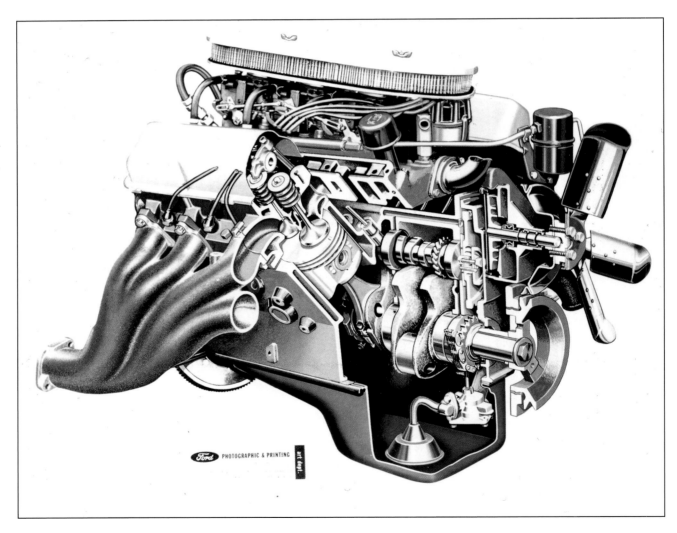

Ford's 1962 406-ci FE big-block V-8 was a brief intermediate step between the 390 and 427. Shown is the six-barrel version more common on the dragstrip and street. Unfortunately for Ford, the 406-powered Galaxie was no match for the 421-ci Pontiac V-8 and the 409 Chevy in NASCAR. Making matters worse, during competition the 406 suffered from cracking engine blocks, to the chagrin of Ford engineers. The next year's 427 solved most of the problems. *Ford*

The Impala Sports Hardtop, with its sloping roofline, was the preferred NASCAR ride in 1962. That year the Impala was still competitive in NASCAR, winning 14 races, but in 1963 GM pulled the rug out from under its factory-backed racing teams with a serious ban on racing.

was Ford's new V-8, the 427 FE big-block, that won the day. Johnson retired from the race with mechanical problems. The top finishing Chevy came in ninth.

As a NASCAR racing engine, the Mark II was strangled in its crib by GM's 1963 edict banning factory-supported racing efforts. This self-imposed pull-out had more teeth behind it than the 1957 AMA voluntary ban, at least as far as management job

security was concerned. Chevy managed eight wins in 1963, but only one in 1964, and was shut out in 1965, 1969, and 1970. Without factory support, Chevrolet's best drivers drifted to other makes. Junior Johnson drove a Dodge in 1964. Pontiac was likewise shut out after 1963.

The Mark II big-block fared better in the long term. Released in Chevrolet passenger cars in 1965

The midyear, 1963-1/2 Galaxie Sports Hardtop models (and corporate cousin Mercury Marauder) yielded aerodynamic gains under high-speed racing conditions thanks to the mild fastback roofline. The cars are also remembered for being the first to receive Ford's 427-ci V-8. The combination cured Ford's stock car racing deficiencies in a hurry. Galaxies won the first five places at the Daytona 500, and won the 1963 manufacturers' championship as well.

at 396 cubic inches, the basic engine design survived into the late 1990s. The 1963 Mark II Chevy spawned no corresponding street musclecar that year, but every Chevy musclecar from the SS396 Camaro, to the SS396 and SS454 Chevelle, to the 427 Corvette can trace its lineage to the stock car mystery motor of 1963.

With Chevy and Pontiac subjected to self-imposed neutering, the interesting engine programs came out of Ford and Chrysler dyno cells for the rest of the decade. While Chevrolet was working on its mystery motor, Ford was working on a surprise of its own. The FE big-block engine family had progressed from the 352 Special of 1960 to the 390 four-barrel and 390 triple two-barrel engines of 1961, to the 406-ci V-8 of 1962. The results were unremarkable. The Fords always seemed to be a step behind Pontiac, Chevy, and Plymouth, in both power output and reliability.

Gus Scussel, who was section supervisor of Ford's racing engine group at the time, had his hands full with the 406. "My first event was the Daytona in 1962, and that engine just didn't have a prayer," he recalled. "Everything broke. Primarily we were losing cylinder blocks. That was the biggest problem. We fixed a lot of things—we worked real close with the Holman-Moody people—but it was just a hopeless case." Specifically, Scussel said, cracks formed in the number two bulkhead in the cylinder block, where the main bearing cap bolted to the block.

Those unpleasant experiences were not wasted. When Ford engineers returned to the drafting table to create the next generation FE racing engine, they made certain they corrected those deficiencies.

The next generation FE came in at 427 cubic inches, although this new big-block was more than just a bore and stroke job. The 427 engine team included Scussel, Don Sullivan, a Ford veteran who had been around so long he had worked on the original flathead Ford V-8 design in the 1930s, Al Rominsky, Bob Schwender, Joe Macura, and supervisor Norm Faustyn.

To improve block rigidity the 1963 427 had cross-bolted main bearing caps, which yielded precise bearing alignment. "Engine speeds that were believed impossible to maintain in large displacement engines are now practical because of the greater crankcase rigidity," Ford explained in their *Total Performance 1903–1963* handbook. Scussel said for the cross-bolted main caps he was inspired by a new International Harvester diesel design, figuring the idea could be adapted to the new high-performance V-8. The 427 used extruded pistons teamed with forged steel connecting rods, another improvement over earlier designs. As with most high-performance V-8s of the day, it had solid lifters and header-style exhaust manifolds. With single four-barrel, as required by NASCAR rules, the 427 produced 410 horsepower. The dual four-barrel

version commonly seen in drag racing was rated at 425 horsepower.

The 427 did its job in making everyone forget about the 406. Together with the new 1963 Sports Hardtop Galaxie, the new engine romped at the Daytona 500, capturing the first five spots. The 427 Galaxie won Ford the NASCAR manufacturers championship that year.

This first version of the 427 was later defined as the "low riser" due to the intake port angles and the engine's overall low profile. Late in 1963 Ford built a "high riser" 427, so named because of its long-runner, tall intake manifold. The low riser was placed in 427 Galaxies destined for the street, while the high riser 427, which required a hood scoop for use, landed in Thunderbolts and Lightweight Galaxies destined for drag racing.

In 1965, Ford released a "medium riser" 427 that combined the high-riser's high-flowing ports and free-breathing characteristics with a lower profile intake manifold that did not require a hood scoop. The medium riser was also blessed with a forged

Dodge returned to NASCAR in 1966 riding on the strength of the fastback Charger and the Hemi engine, finally available in street form. The radical fastback shape didn't endear the car to everyone, but it was swoopy enough to earn the NASCAR drivers' championship for David Pearson.

Dodge's first attempt at seriously cleaning up the Charger's aerodynamics was the 1969 500 model. Dodge eliminated the recessed nose by mounting a grille pilfered from the Coronet R/T flush with the edge of the hood and fenders. *DaimlerChrysler Corporate Historical Collection*

Dodge farmed out the Charger 500's special bodywork to Creative Industries. The company raised the rear glass and filled in the tunnel-roof section to clean up the rear airflow over the Charger. The main identifying mark for the Charger 500 was the "bumblebee stripe," similar to the one used on the R/T, but with a numeral 500 instead of the R/T designation. Dodge managed to fool NASCAR on the 500's production status. Only 392 were built, instead of the 500 minimum. *DaimlerChrysler Corporate Historical Collection*

steel crankshaft and "side oiler" lubrication system that featured large oil passages machined into the side of the block. The side oiler layout solved a problem the 427s had with getting oil to the bearings.

Of all the early-to-mid-1960s stock car-inspired musclecars (the 409 Chevy, the 421 Super Duty Pontiac, the "Max Wedge" Mopar big-blocks), the production

1963 and 1964 427 Galaxies were probably built in the largest numbers for the general public.

The 427 might have turned out to be just another stepping stone had Ford's plans for 1965 panned out. The introduction of Chrysler's 426 Hemi in 1964 shocked Ford into responding. The next step in the FE big-block evolution was the single overhead

Anyone bold—or confident—enough to drive a Dodge Charger Daytona on the street was usually greeted by perplexed stares of amazement. It was not a car for introverts. Standard power was the 375-horsepower 440 four-barrel V-8; the 425-horse, 426-ci Hemi was optional. *Mike Mueller*

cam (SOHC) 427, an exotic hemi head powerplant with great performance potential. NASCAR shot down the "Cammer" 427 as just another expensive toy from Ford's racing department—and they were right. Even Ford couldn't stretch the definition of a "production" engine to include the Cammer. The SOHC 427 was never installed in a production vehicle. All the engines built were sold over the counter, primarily to racers. With NASCAR's rejection, the Cammer big-block made all its history in drag racing competition.

Chrysler's Hemi-head V-8s made a big impact during two decades, the 1950s and 1960s. The original Hemi burned up NASCAR in the 1950s. The Chrysler 300 series scored 27 NASCAR Grand National wins in 1955, 22 in 1956.

The revived 1960s Hemi V-8 shared some of its architecture with the earlier 331–392-ci Hemis, but

was essentially its own animal, a combination of the wedge-head V-8 shortblock with a new Hemi cylinder head. It was certainly meant for racing, not just providing a kick in the seat for drivers of Chrysler's luxury cars, as the earlier Hemis had done. Chrysler engineers were told the deadline for the engine was the 1964 Daytona 500. The Hemi's displacement was 426 cubic inches, just under the NASCAR and NHRA limits. Its hemispherical combustion chambers were extremely efficient, and promoted good power production. As with most performance V-8s of the day, it came with a solid lifter cam, header-style exhaust manifolds, and beefy items like a double roller timing chain.

The 426 Hemi made its stock car debut on February 23, 1964, at Daytona. Richard Petty led a first through third sweep, scoring his first superspeedway victory en route to the 1964 Championship. In the

Buddy Baker was one of Dodge's Daytona pilots in 1969. He's shown here with Union 76 "RaceStoppers" Ann Romeo (center) and Cheryl Johnson. The trio are pictured at the inaugural NASCAR race at Texas International Speedway, which explains the cowboy hat and spurs.

Hemi's debut year, Plymouths won 12 races, Dodges 14.

The engine certainly made an impression on Petty. "I had driven a lot of hot cars before, and I sure have since, but I've never been in anything that felt quite like the hemi," he wrote in *King Richard I: The Autobiography of America's Greatest Auto Racer* (1986, with William Neely). "The power was there all the time; it didn't matter when you punched it, it socked you back in your seat. It sounded like it was going to suck the hood in."

This quick success came at a price. Chrysler got caught in the same web that had snared the 1963 Chevy mystery motor and the Ford 427 SOHC—its status, or lack of it, as a production engine. At least Chrysler could make an arguable case in favor of its engine. Technically, it was possible to purchase a new Dodge or Plymouth automobile with the engine installed from the factory, provided you were a racer, and Chrysler wanted you to have one.

But there was no street-tuned version of the engine that year, and on those grounds NASCAR banned the Hemi. Chrysler, in a major corporate snit, pulled out of NASCAR stock car racing for 1965. The situation produced the odd spectacle of Richard Petty spending the 1965 season drag racing in a Petty Blue Barracuda. With GM and Chrysler out of racing for their various reasons, it came as no surprise that Ford won 48 of 55 Grand National races that year.

Detroit was willing to go to great lengths to win races, however, so in August 1965 a "street Hemi" debuted in 1966 models. The 426 Hemi became a regular production option in the Dodge Charger and Coronet, and Plymouth Belvedere I and Satellite. The street Hemi differed from the 1964 and 1965 race versions mainly in that it ran a lower compression ratio, had cast iron exhaust manifolds, a camshaft with less lift and duration, and inline four-barrel Carter carbs in place of the Holleys mounted on a cross-ram. It was rated at 425 horsepower, the same as the race engines.

Chrysler welcomed themselves back to NASCAR with 16 Plymouth victories and 18 Dodge wins in 1966. Richard Petty's record in 1967 was astounding: 27 victories, including a stretch of 10 in a row. He coasted to his second Grand National championship.

A Clean Hole Through the Atmosphere

Aerodynamic performance was a much bigger factor in stock car racing than in drag racing, and the automakers sought this avenue for an edge over the competition. Attempts to clean up aerodynamics were sometimes crude, as modern wind tunnel technology was still a gleam in racers' eyes. Much "aerodynamic" design was measured by eye, or compromised by assembly line limitations.

One factor in the 1961 Chevy's success was the sport coupe body style, with its sloping roofline. The new 427 engine was crucial to Ford's 1963 racing success, but so was the Ford sports hardtop body style, also seen on the Mercury Marauder.

Sloping C-pillars made for an attractive car and helped at the track, but by the mid-1960s the

Bobby Isaac won the 1970 NASCAR season title in the #71 Daytona, the winged wonder's sole NASCAR championship. He's shown here at Riverside that year. Isaac went on to set top speed records at Bonneville in the Daytona. *Bob Tronolone*

The extreme fastback rooflines of the Ford Talladega and Mercury Cyclone Spoiler gave the cars a natural aerodynamic advantage at the track. The extended noses and flush grilles of the two cleaned up the airflow around the front ends, although the Mercury's design proved to be slightly more aerodynamic thanks to the Cyclone's hoodline. Pictured front and center is LeeRoy Yarbrough's Torino Talladega; on the far side is the Wood Brothers' Mercury Cyclone of Cale Yarborough. David Pearson's championship-winning Talladega is in the background. *Texas Department of Transportation*

attempts to cheat the wind were much more obvious. The 1966 Dodge Charger used such an extreme fastback roofline it nearly qualified as a flatback. The design was not perfect, as the Charger had a problem with rear-end lift, but the combination of 426 Hemi and fastback Charger helped David Pearson win the NASCAR drivers title in 1966. For 1967 Dodge offered a small rear deck spoiler option for the production Charger, which allowed it to be used in competition. The spoiler helped a bit with the Charger's rear-end lift problem.

Going against popular wisdom about "win on Sunday, sell on Monday," the race wins and Hemi engines did not endear the Charger to the public. The extreme fastback was the obvious culprit. And the Hemi, street tune or not, was hardly a practical engine for everyday use. Dodge sold 37,300 Chargers in 1966, but only 15,788 in 1967.

The redesigned 1968 Charger was far more popular with the public. The new car looked aerodynamic, full of handsome curves and a pinched "coke-bottle" waist, but wasn't that much of an improvement.

Some of the features that looked so stylish on the street car, such as the recessed grille and "tunnel back" rear glass, dirtied the airflow at high speed.

Ford's aerodynamic efforts were much more effective in 1968. The restyled Torino and Mercury Cyclone had radical fastback sheet metal of their own, called a "SportsRoof" in Ford terminology. The SportsRoof featured one sloping roofline from the top of the windshield to the end of the trunk lid. Ford had scored a few important victories in the previous years—Mario Andretti won the 1967 Daytona 500 in a 427 Fairlane—but after Pearson's championship in 1966 and Richard Petty's dominating performance in 1967, it was a given that the intermediate Fairlane and Torino would get sheet metal optimized for stock car racing.

And win they did. The 1968 Torino won the NASCAR, USAC, and ARCA (Automobile Racing Club of America) stock car champions, thanks largely to the SportsRoof styling. The capable Ford drivers that

The Mercury Cyclone Spoiler II had slightly more rear overhang than the Talladega, contributing to its aerodynamic edge. The Dan Gurney edition carried a blue and white color scheme. The Spoiler was the second Mercury to honor versatile racer Gurney; a Cougar XR-7 G had been the first. *Mike Mueller photo*

A Daytona takes on fuel at the Texas 500 Grand National race on December 7, 1969. Dodge drivers started the season in the wingless Charger 500, but later switched to the new Daytona in order to keep up with the Fords and Mercurys. The air-extracting fender scoops on the Daytona allowed the front end to be lowered while maintaining tire clearance. *Texas Department of Transportation*

year included NASCAR champ David Pearson in a Fairlane, and Cale Yarborough in a Wood Brothers Mercury.

In the early part of the decade, the emphasis had been on building suitably large and powerful production engines for stock car racing, with aerodynamics as a bonus. In the late 1960s, however the focus shifted to building special production-car bodies that could give a manufacturer an edge on the track.

The top street Torino and Cyclone models were both named GT, and were nothing special, until the 428 CJ engine option came on line midyear. But Dodge's response to the Torino and Cyclone racing success was definitely a break from tradition. The 1969 Dodge Charger 500 was sent out into the world with aerodynamic enhancements intended solely for the high banks. Racing success had

become such a priority in Detroit that the effort and expense required to produce a limited number of street cars with special stock car-friendly sheet metal was shrugged off.

Dodge farmed out the Charger 500 project to Creative Industries. To clean up the airflow, the recessed Charger grille and hide-away headlamps were eliminated, replaced by a flush grille with exposed headlamps. The tunnel-back rear glass design was also replaced. Creative Industries raised the backlight and smoothed-in the body contours, creating a clean roofline. As evidence of the Charger 500's genetic predisposition for racing, the cars were sold to the general public with shortcomings that would never have passed muster in other times, such as a severely reduced trunk opening, a by-product of the extended roofline. The Charger

Plymouth created its own version of the Charger Daytona, the Road Runner-based Superbird, largely to lure Richard Petty back from Ford. From a racing standpoint, it was a good investment. Petty scored 18 of Plymouth's 21 victories in 1970. Petty is shown here at Riverside in 1970. *Bob Tronolone photo*

500 was sold with the 440 V-8 standard, the 426 Hemi optional.

"You've got to hand it to the Chrysler guys: if they race it, they also sell it," noted *Hot Rod's* Steve Kelly in a Charger 500 review. "That really doesn't make them heroes, but it does help promote the image of stock car racing. When you can buy your race car, or at least the basics of one, through a dealership, you're a lot closer to racing *real* stock cars."

(A note to avoid confusion: Dodge offered a different Charger 500 model beginning in 1970. It was merely a regular Charger with a few upgraded features. The aero-minded 500 was produced only in 1969.)

On the track, the Charger 500 performed better than the regular Charger, but still wasn't as effective as the Fords. Worse, the Charger 500 created a little friction in the Chrysler camp. Only Dodge had received a special aero model, not Plymouth's Road Runner. Between the Fords and the Charger 500, Plymouth drivers like Richard Petty, only two seasons removed from a championship, were left in the slow lane.

continued on page 61

Next page: Plymouth Superbirds were sold with vinyl tops to hide the scars from the rear glass modifications. Large "Plymouth" billboard graphics and Road Runner decals on the wing only added to the car's flamboyant personality. Hood pins were standard.

The Boss 429 Racing Connection

The Boss 429 Mustang was a by-product of Ford's desire to race the semi-hemi engine in NASCAR. In order to qualify the engine for competition it had to be a production engine, and a Boss '9 Mustang was deemed by the company to be more marketable than a Boss 429 Torino. Both car and engine were produced during 1969 and 1970 only.

Ford built the Boss 429 V-8 as a replacement NASCAR engine for the 427 FE big block. How then did the engine end up in a Mustang? In a word: marketing.

The Boss 429 V-8 was built specifically with stock car racing in mind. Inspired more than a little by the Chrysler 426 Hemi, the Boss 429 had crescent-shaped combustion chambers, a so-called "semi Hemi" design. To promote high-rpm breathing the heads had massive ports and valves, a strategy also used on the Boss 302. The engine didn't use head gaskets, but O-rings around the cylinders.

For Ford to run the Boss 429 in NASCAR it had to put the engine into production. The Torino and Mercury Cyclone were the Ford Motor Company entries in NASCAR, but it was decided a Boss 429 Mustang would be more marketable than the family-oriented Torino. It was not an unreasonable decision, given that Mustang high-performance models routinely outsold their Torino-based counterparts. And as far as NASCAR was concerned, it didn't matter which car the engine came in as long as it was a regular production piece the general public could order.

The Boss 429 took a little while to catch on with racers. The 427 FE V-8 was a proven winner, while the Boss '9's early performance raised some durability concerns. Eventually the Boss 429 won out, although it had a short life itself in stock car circles.

Boss 429 Mustangs were assembled at Kar Kraft in Brighton, Michigan, in 1969 and 1970. The engine was, naturally, detuned for the street. The pedestrian Boss had its own block casting, smaller intake valves, a milder cam, and smaller four-barrel carburetor. It was rated at 375 horsepower.

Although certainly a fast car, the performance of a stock Boss 429 Mustang never quite lived up to all the expectations generated by the engine's spec sheet. A well-tuned Mach 1 with the far cheaper 428 CJ was easily the equal of a Boss 429 in most situations. Even with the detuning, the massive ports were still impractical for street use, producing an engine that preferred high rpm to low-speed grunt. Of course, a few modifications woke the engine up—it was, after all, built for racing.

The Boss 429 V-8 is instantly recognizable thanks to its distinctive rocker covers. It was a race engine from the beginning, and required considerable detuning for street use. The production version was rated at 375 horsepower.

The Superbird featured a tunnel between the core support and nose piece to direct air to the engine. The system worked well enough on the race car, but street Superbirds were notorious for running hot—unless the owner liked triple-digit speeds. The 440-ci four-barrel V-8 was standard equipment.

Since the Superbird's unique nose precluded the use of a bumper jack, the street models came standard with a special scissors jack for the front, as well as a bumper jack for the rear. The arrangement was one of many compromises Superbird ownership required.

Continued from page 57

"Ford had caught up with the hemis," Petty recalled in his autobiography. "They had Cale Yarborough and LeeRoy Yarbrough, who were burning up tracks everywhere. The races they didn't win in a Ford, David Pearson did. I still managed to win sixteen races during the 1968 season, but Chrysler didn't make it any easier come contract time. They wouldn't honor any of our requests, particularly to drive a Dodge, which was more aerodynamic, so we decided it might be time to listen to Ford."

Winning over Richard Petty was a huge coup for Ford. But the company had another trick up its sleeve. Ford, too, was working on a special aerodynamic model. Named after the newly constructed Talladega Superspeedway in Alabama, the Torino Talladega first ran down the assembly line in January and February of 1969.

With a swoopy fastback already in place, Ford focused on the Fairlane's nose for improvement. Like the Charger, the stock Fairlane and Torino had a recessed grille that junked up the airflow at speed. Ford's solution was a long, drooping nose piece with a flush grille. The Talladega was fitted with a small front bumper fabricated from an altered rear bumper. The rocker panel sheet metal was rolled under, which allowed Ford to lower the car, further improving aerodynamics.

To homologate the Talladega, a version was sold to the general public, naturally. The street editions were available in either Wimbledon White, Royal Maroon, or Presidential Blue colors, with a matte black hood to reduce glare. The cars came standard with a 335-horsepower 428 CJ, C-6 automatic transmission, and 3.25:1 axle ratio. The Talladega was fairly low key, with a faux gas cap with stylized "T" being the most apparent identification. Approximately 745 were built, including prototypes.

Mercury was likewise given an aero model, named the Cyclone Spoiler II. Like the Talladega most of the work was done on the nose, but, as its name implied, the Mercury Spoiler II also had a rear deck spoiler. The long-nosed race Spoiler II was sold to the public as either a red and white-striped Cale

The Charger Daytona's wing was painted in contrasting colors, similar to the Dodge R/T "bumblebee" stripe. Street-bound Plymouth Superbirds had body-colored rear wings. The Superbird wing was the taller of the two.

optioned with Mercury's larger big-block engines. Ford also had a separate performance model positioned between the Torino GT and the Talladega. The Fairlane Cobra was designed to compete with the cut-rate Plymouth Road Runner, a musclecar devoid of frills but packed with go-fast hardware. It came standard with the 335-horse 428 Cobra Jet. Ford played up the Cobra's link to racing Torinos, too. "This 1969 Boss Snake is blood brother to the specially modified Torinos that let it all hang out on this year's NASCAR circuit," Ford ads reminded enthusiasts in late 1968 advertising.

With the Charger 500 proving unequal to the task of beating the Fords and Mercurys in NASCAR, Dodge took a giant step out of the automotive mainstream. Its next aero car was so extreme that the surviving examples still draw astonished reactions when viewed by the public even today. The 1969 Dodge Charger Daytona was 1960s high-performance excess wrapped up in one eye-ball grabbing package.

The Charger Daytona is remembered for its two most noticeable features—a towering wing and long pointed nose. Instead of a flush nose as used on the Charger 500, the Daytona's nose jutted outward to an 18-inch long tapered snout. Dodge built the nose pieces out of metal, and incorporated pop-up headlamps for street use. The Charger 500's sloping roofline was retained, and teamed with an almost comically tall adjustable aluminum wing designed for maximum downforce at high speed. Small, reverse-mounted scoops were mounted over air-extracting holes cut into the fenders. As with the Charger 500, the special parts were installed at Creative Industries in Detroit.

The Charger Daytona made its racing debut at Talladega Superspeedway in September 1969, and by then Plymouth had seen enough. Petty recalled in his autobiography that Plymouth was ready to build an aero car of its own. "At the end of the [1969] season," Petty wrote, "Chrysler came to us and said 'Don't you guys think it's about time you come home?'"

"'Will you listen to some of our requests?' I asked."

"'You name it,' they said."

"We went home."

Obviously, one of those requests was for an aerodynamic car like the Charger Daytona or Ford Talladega, which Plymouth delivered in 1970 in

Yarborough edition or a blue and white Dan Gurney edition. Oddly enough, the street Spoiler II came standard with the 351 Windsor four-barrel V-8, rated at 290 horsepower, rather than the 428. Not so oddly, the Mercury had a generally plusher interior than the stripped-down Talladegas.

Confusing matters somewhat was that Mercury built another Spoiler model in 1969, this one without the special nose, but with rear wing intact. Called the Cyclone Spoiler, it was sold in the same Gurney and Yarborough paint schemes, but could be

Ford had its corporate hand in just about every form of racing in the 1960s. During the decade, Ford-powered vehicles won the Indy 500 three times, the 24 Hours of LeMans sports car race back-to-back, the SCCA Trans-Am title twice, plus assorted stock car and drag racing titles. Ford was not shy about advertising these facts, as this insert in a car enthusiasts magazine of the day attests. Jacque Passino led the effort as special vehicles manager of the Product Development Group, a fancy title for "racing boss."

the form of the Superbird. Plymouth was remarkably up-front about the whole deal. "It's not the only reason Richard returned to Plymouth, but you can put it at the top of the list," stated a Plymouth ad from the spring of 1970. It was no small commitment, as NASCAR had changed its homoligation rules for 1970, increasing the number of cars an automaker needed to build from 500 to 2,000 in order for that model to be classified as a production car.

At first glance the Superbird was nearly identical to the Charger Daytona, but there were differences. The Superbird was based on the 1970 Road Runner, although it used Dodge Coronet fenders

and hood. The nose piece swept down a bit further, and the car used an even taller rear wing, at an even more extreme angle. The Superbird came standard with the 375-horsepower 440 four-barrel V-8, with the 390-horse 440 Six Pack and 425-horse Hemi optional.

Buying a Charger Daytona or Superbird for street use was a seriously optimistic act. Buyers had to be willing to put up with incredulous stares and outright laughter. And forget about downtown parking spaces.

Car dealers bore a burden too. Daytonas and Superbirds were known to sit unsold for as long as a year. It was not at all unusual for a dealer to strip off the wing and retrofit a production front end, and sell the cars as a regular Charger or Road Runner. Few people, even car buffs, wanted such a freakish-looking car for daily transportation. Besides the looks issue, the cars were expensive. The factory ADP (Advertised Dealer Price) for a Superbird was $4,298, which was a full $1,000 more than a Road Runner convertible. A Plymouth GTX, a pretty nice car in its own right, was priced at $3,535.

There were additional burdens to bear. The aerodynamic nose piece that worked so well on the track proved to be a liability around town. At speed the design efficiently funneled air into the engine compartment, but cruising around town the Daytona Charger and Superbird suffered from cooling problems. The Superbird's trunk couldn't even open fully, limiting utility.

But the outrageous winged cars accomplished what they were supposed too. Bobby Isaac won the 1970 NASCAR championship behind the wheel of a 1969 Daytona. Richard Petty was happy. It was all about wins, baby.

Following on the success of the Talladega, Ford nearly escalated the aero car war to another level in 1970. In the spring and summer of 1969 the company worked on a King Cobra design for the restyled 1970 Torino. The upcoming car had a slick fastback roofline, but another recessed grille, and a concave rear glass. Stylist Larry Shinoda worked up an elongated nose for the Torino, not unlike that employed by Chrysler.

The King Cobra was never produced for a variety of reasons. In part, Ford was scared off by NASCAR's new production minimums. There was serious discussion at Ford about whether the company could sell 2,000 of the ungainly cars. Additionally, testing proved the car needed a serious rear spoiler to reduce lift at high speed. The company declined, and the era of special aero cars built for stock car racing came to ân end.

TRANS-AM, A PLACE FOR PONYCARS

While intermediate- and full-sized musclecars tore up the NASCAR tracks and NHRA dragstrips in the mid-1960s, the newly categorized "ponycars" fell somewhere between. In 1964 the Mustang and Barracuda started the whole long hood/short deck/compact size/sporty image amalgam that was categorized as the ponycar class. Just where they fit into the overall racing scheme was the question of the day.

Although certainly drag raced, the small V-8 engines in the Mustang and Barracuda guaranteed the cars would never dominate the top Super Stock classes, where horsepower generated by massive big-blocks was paramount. Most early ponycars slugged it out in F/Stock, or as wild exhibition freak shows, like the Hurst "Hemi Under Glass" rear-engined 1965 Barracuda. NASCAR later formed a sedan racing class, but the top Grand National division—and the spotlight—was reserved for the larger cars.

The most comfortable fit for the ponycars was in the Sports Car Club of America (SCCA). The fledgling ponycars were not sports cars in the truest sense, and their economy-car suspensions were hardly reminiscent of Europe's finest, but the smaller, lighter vehicles nonetheless found a home on twisty road courses.

One of the first to come to that conclusion was Carroll Shelby. His 1965 GT350 Mustang was delivered straight from the Shelby plant in virtual road racing form. One of Shelby's factory team GT350Rs, driven by Jerry Titus, won the SCCA's 1965 B-Production Class Championship.

The 1969 Z28s were the last to use the 302-ci engine, and the last to dominate the Trans-Am series (until the 1980s). They were also the most popular of the early Z28s, with production above 20,000.

Jim Whelan, behind the wheel of his 1966 Shelbyized Trans-Am Mustang, in 1967. Whelan said the Mustang was very competitive early in the series. His car, like many early Mustangs, was patterned after the Shelby GT-350R. The car ran Shelby Tri-Y headers, "because that's about all there was," Whelan said. Whelan described the Mustang as basically a notchback GT-350R. *Jim Whelan*

For its part, after years running amateur-only events, the SCCA decided to sanction professional races in 1961. The idea of a professional sedan-based racing class progressed in fits and starts, finally kicking into gear in 1966 with the Trans-American Sedan Championship. The series was divided into an Under-2-liter class, designed with European cars such as Alfa Romeos and BMWs in mind, and an Over-2-liter class. In that first year the Over-2-liter class was mostly filled with Mustangs, Dodge Darts, Plymouth Barracudas, and Chevrolet Corvairs.

The SCCA adopted FIA homologation standards, meaning cars that ran in the series had to be actual production cars using parts available to the general public. The rules also held engine displacements to a 305-ci limit. This helped some manufacturers, and hurt others. Ford already had a 289-ci V-8, with a 302 on the drawing board for 1968. The Mopars ran solid little 273-ci V-8s early on, but later had to run destroked 340s. Pontiac's smallest V-8 came in at 326 ci, though, causing them problems when they entered the series with the Firebird. When Chevrolet's

Camaro debuted, the company had to create a special engine, the Z28's 302, in order to qualify.

Initially there was no driver's championship, only a manufacturers' championship, which made the cars the stars. Even without a drivers' title, though, the Trans-Am attracted America's best drivers. Dan Gurney, Parnelli Jones, Mark Donohue, David Pearson, and Peter Revson all spent time in the Trans-Am series. The Trans-Am appealed to drivers for many reasons, not least of which was a paycheck. But the chance to showcase the ponycars in a rapidly progressing series was irresistible to the auto manufacturers, and as the Trans-Am grew in popularity, they hired the best guns around to race their products.

The first Trans-Am race was held in March, 1966 at Sebring, in Florida. Jochen Rindt won in an Alfa GTA, with Bob Tullius' Dart taking second overall and first in Over-2-liter. In June, the Mustang scored its first victory, with Bob Johnson and Tom Yeager at the wheel, at Mid-America Raceway. Ford won the inaugural Over 2-liter championship, while Alfa Romeo won the first Under-2-liter manufacturers' trophy.

Ground Level

The Trans-Am series hardly started as big-time racing. The first few races passed largely unnoticed. Competitors definitely did not rely on racing purses to make a living, and pit crews usually consisted of what buddies could be dragged along. Things did not stay that way for long, but the early days of the Trans-Am were fairly uncomplicated.

Jim Whelan was typical of those early racers. Taking experience gained from racing a 1963 Corvette split-window coupe in regional events, he competed part-time in SCCA A-Sedan and Trans-Am from 1967 to 1972, teamed with Dick Roe. Although not a "factory" driver, he was representative of the do-it-yourself ethos of the early days. He witnessed the changes in the series, from nearly-stock cars racing for glory to money-rich factory teams racing for bragging rights.

Whelan's first Trans-Am ride was in a 1966 Mustang GT coupe with a Shelby-prepped Hi-Po 289, followed by a 1967 Mustang, and finally a Boss 302. Sponsorship was rare in the early days, but Whelan worked a deal with Tousley Ford in White Bear Lake, Minnesota. He was able to purchase his 1966 Mustang for cost. He also received support from the Mustang Clubs of America Midwest region. (It helped that Tousley Ford was headquarters for the Twin Cities Mustang Club.) In the Mustang's first couple of years on the market, Ford backed the Mustang clubs whenever possible, hoping to build loyalty to the brand.

Whelan entered his first Trans-Am race in August 1967, at Continental Divide raceway. He remembers the early days of the Trans-Am as being fairly informal. "Everybody was volunteer," he said. "We worked normal jobs during the day, got off work, came home, changed clothes, went to the shop and worked on the car until 12 or one in the morning. And then more often than not stopped at the local bar and grille afterwards."

As with any racing series, there was a learning curve. "The rules were really strict back then," Whelan said. "We interpreted them maybe a little stricter than they were. So we were always maybe just a tad bit behind. Once we got into a couple of the Trans-Am races, we got to talking to people and found out what you could get away with and what you couldn't get away with."

As for that first Mustang, it was a fine example of how close to stock the typical early Trans-Am cars

Besides his GT-350 Mustangs for the street, Shelby also built race cars for his own team and for customers. He built 26 notchback Mustangs, including the car pictured, in 1967 for use in SCCA Trans-Am and A-sedan racing. One just like it, driven by Jerry Titus, won the championship for Ford in 1967.

were. "It just had a roll bar in it. We moved the battery to the trunk, and put a Detroit Locker and gears in it, bought wheels and tires. I mean, the first two races we ran it in we had the stock exhaust manifolds," he recalled. "We pulled the motor and went through that to the limit of the rules. We put a bigger radiator in, and later we added an oil cooler. But it was basically strip the interior out, put a roll bar in—you didn't have to have a full cage—and go racing."

What factory backing there was from Ford for the independent drivers came primarily through the network of Ford dealers, or indirectly through Shelby American and stock car veteran Bud Moore's shop in Spartanburg, South Carolina. "Back then a privateer had a very good chance of placing very high," Whelan said. "The privateers could afford to compete with the factories, because the rules were so limiting."

When support came it was rarely in the form of money, but as advice, parts, or machine work at very good prices through Bud Moore or Shelby American. "We got a lot of good, cheap tires through Firestone," Whelan said. "We were one of the few teams running Firestone tires. Champion was always there. 'What do you need? Here, let me check your plugs.' They'd come around and seek you out. . . . You'd come in from a practice run, and the Firestone man would be over there and the Champion spark plug man would be over there,

and while you're doing minor chassis adjustments, they'd be checking your plugs and looking at your tires, making recommendations."

Street Spawn

In 1967 the Trans-Am series started to gain steam. The schedule expanded from seven races in 1966 to 12. And as crowds grew and more ponycars were thrust into the marketplace, it was inevitable that the series would spawn special production models. After all, the SCCA's rules allowed relatively few modifications, so a regular production car that closely fit the Trans-Am template would have a huge advantage.

The new ponycars that year were Chevrolet's Camaro, Pontiac's Firebird, and Mercury's Cougar. All followed the Mustang blueprint, the Camaro most directly. Pontiac strove to give the Firebird a more international flair, while the Cougar, loaded with luxuries and sound deadener, was pitched at a more upscale buyer.

The Camaro, as introduced, came with either 327-ci, 350-ci, or, later, 396-ci V-8s—all of which were too large for Trans-Am. Chevrolet was still officially out of racing, with corporate policy forbidding factory participation or advertising of racing feats. But Vince Piggins, Chevrolet's product promotion manager, knew that it was crucial for the Camaro to at least be part of the game. The Camaro was designed to steal some of the youth market away from Mustang, which meant it had to have a presence at the track to have any credibility on the street.

After running experiments with highly tuned 283-ci Camaro prototypes, Chevrolet finalized a Trans-Am package late in 1966. The new option was named "Z28," with the alphanumeric designation coming from the package's option code. The Z28 option was released well after the Camaro's Fall 1966 introduction, but in plenty of time for the 1967 racing season.

Starting with a 327 block fitted with a 283 crankshaft, Chevrolet created a 302-ci engine used exclusively in the Z28. The 302 housed a machine shop's worth of heavy-duty

A typical Shelby Trans-Am 289-ci engine ran GT-40 cylinder heads, aluminum high-rise intake with dual four-barrels, Cobra R headers, and fabricated air box.

The Camaro Z28 debuted midway through the 1967 model year. Other than its twin racing stripes, it carried no external identification, and few knew of its availability. Roger Penske knew, however, and put it toward its intended use—Trans-Am racing. *Chevrolet*

equipment, like a forged crankshaft and connecting rods, a solid-lifter cam, large 2.02-inch intake valves and 1.60-inch exhaust valves, an aluminum intake manifold topped by a 780 cfm Holley carburetor, and a free-flowing exhaust. The compression ratio was an octane-squeezing 11.0:1. Options included a cold air induction package that sucked air in from the windshield cowl, and headers supplied loose for customer installation. The 302 was rated at 290 horsepower at a sky-high (for an American car) 5,800 rpm.

The suspension was likewise Trans-Am oriented. The Z28 came with heavy duty springs and shocks, Quick Ratio steering, and 15x6-inch wheels. Checking the Z28 option box required ordering the close-ratio four-speed transmission, as well as one of the Camaro's available brake upgrades. The Z28 option added $358 to the window sticker, plus the cost of the mandatory options.

On the street, the 1967 Z28 maintained a stealthy presence. Only 602 were built, and the cars

Next page: The Z28 Camaro was a perfect example of Detroit building a barely streetable car for the sole purpose of qualifying it for production status, thereby allowing it to be raced. The Z28's blueprint was practically lifted from the Trans-Am rulebook. The 302-ci small-block fit just under the SCCA's displacement limit, and was used exclusively in the Z28. Its high-revving state of tune made for a cranky street engine, but was ideal for racing. The Z28 also came with a heavy-duty radiator, quick-ratio steering, and a close-ratio four-speed transmission—all necessary for competition.
Next page, inset: Chevrolet created the Z28's special 302 engine by fitting the 283 crankshaft to the 327 block. With racing in mind, the 302 came with a forged-steel crankshaft and connecting rods, a windage tray, a solid-lifter cam, a high-rise aluminum intake manifold, an 800 cfm Holley carburetor, and an 11.0:1 compression ratio. The fiberglass plenum air intake system was optional. Chevrolet rated the engine at an amusing 290 horsepower.

After dominating in 1968, Mark Donohue found himself in a tight battle with Parnelli Jones for the SCCA Trans-Am championship in 1969. Donohue won six races that year, including Laguna Seca, in August, pictured here. *Bob Tronolone*

carried no external "Z28" identification. Only two wide racing stripes along the hood and decklid gave the game away.

The Z28's track success propelled the car into the spotlight. Roger Penske was the first to embrace the Z28, backing his effort with an extremely professional race team, relatively generous Sunoco sponsorship, and the talented Mark Donohue as driver. The distinctive blue and yellow Sunoco Camaros stood out from the crowd, and soon earned a loyal fan following.

In August 1967, Mark Donohue and Craig Fisher teamed to score the Camaro's first Trans-Am win, at Marlboro Speedway. The Penske Z28 scored two more wins that year, but Jerry Titus drove Ford to the manufacturers championship in a Shelby-built Mustang.

By the following year the world was certainly aware of the Z28. Even without the televised race coverage so common today, the Penske/Donohue

Z28s earned their share of notoriety. Plus, seemingly every car magazine in the free world got its hands on a production 1968 Z28, making for some entertaining reading. *Road & Track*, in their 1968 test of a Camaro Z28, saw right through Chevrolet's "racing ban" subterfuge. "Who says GM isn't racing? If the Z-28 isn't a bona fide racing car—in street clothes for this test—then we've never seen one," they opined.

With the 302 V-8's power band on the high end of the tachometer, it was obvious the Z28's street manners were a secondary concern. "The engine makes no bones about its character. It idles lumpily at 900 rpm and has very little torque below 4000 rpm, considering the car's great weight (3355 lbs.)," they wrote. "Chevrolet obviously achieved what they set out to do—namely, build a race-winning Trans-Am sedan."

Penske's efforts bore fruit in 1968, when Donohue won 10 of the 13 Trans-Am races that season, scoring more than twice as many points as the nearest competitor. He repeated as champion again in 1969 in a close-fought battle with Parnelli Jones, winning 6 of 12. By then the competition between the factory-backed teams was intense, leading to all sorts of "innovations" and creative interpretation of the rules. One of the innovations from the Penske team included using dry ice to pack the gasoline. As Mark Donohue explained in a Chevrolet-produced Trans-Am documentary, "We calculated that by freezing the gas and reducing its temperature roughly 40 to 50 degrees, we could fit 23 gallons into the 22 gallon tank," he said.

If Chevrolet wanted to build a credible street reputation through racing heroics, the Z28 certainly delivered. Chevrolet built 7,199 Z28s in 1968, and 20,302 in 1969, showing that the Trans-Am Camaros spread their influence well beyond the Trans-Am paddock.

Sign of the Cat

Another member of the SCCA Trans-Am class of 1967 was the Mercury Cougar. Although its day in the Trans-Am racing limelight was brief, it made a big impact.

Ford's Mercury division threw everything it had into the effort. It signed Bud Moore's very capable race shop to run the factory team Cougars, employing such drivers as Dan Gurney, David Pearson, 1963 Indy 500 winner Parnelli Jones, Peter Revson, Ed Leslie, and Cale Yarborough.

Moore's team ran the Cougar GT model with a high-performance 289 V-8. Not surprising, considering the two cars' common fundamentals, the Bud Moore Cougars ran race setups similar to that of the Mustang teams. Despite the Cougars' handicap of being less aerodynamic and heavier than the Mustangs, the Mercury ponycar nearly dethroned its Ford counterpart in the manufacturers' championship.

The first Cougar victory in 1967 provided arguably the most memorable finish in Trans-Am history. Dan Gurney beat Parnelli Jones at Green Valley Raceway, in the closest finish on record—only 3 feet separated

first from second. Peter Revson later drove a Cougar to victories at Lime Rock and Bryar, and David Pearson took the checkered at Riverside for his lone Trans-Am win.

The Cougars gave Mercury a second-place finish in the 1967 manufacturer's championship, a mere two points behind Ford. Ultimately, that success hurt the Mercury Trans-Am effort, as corporate decision makers decided that funding a Ford versus Mercury deathmatch was not the best use for the racing dollars. Mercury pulled its factory backing for the 1968 season, and would largely steer clear of the Trans-Am series until the 1980s.

But one street Cougar did spin off from Mercury's Trans-Am effort, the XR-7G. The XR-7 was Mercury's top-line luxury model, while the "G" stood for Dan Gurney. The XR-7G was more a commemorative piece, a way to capitalize on Dan Gurney's popularity, than a special model built specifically for Trans-Am racing. It was, nonetheless, yet another musclecar with its origins based in racing.

On top of plush XR-7 trim, the G equipment included simulated hood scoops, hood lock pins, fog lamps, and racing mirrors. Large C-pillar medallions with "G" in the center were the primary identification. Several of these also received sunroofs from the American Sunroof Company.

For a company that supposedly wasn't involved in racing, Chevrolet sure made a lot of parts suitable only for the race track. In 1969 they released this crossram intake manifold as a dealer-installed option. It was totally unsuitable for the street, but produced good high-rpm power for Trans-Am racing. The system used two 600 cfm Holleys.

In 1969 the Z28 got the cowl-induction hood with engine identification. Twin hood stripes were a Z28 trademark during its early years.

American Made

Prior to 1968, American Motors' attempts to woo the youth market had been limited to appealing to thrifty (or broke) young adults with dressed-up Rambler Americans, or with the odd fastback Marlin. But a corporate strategy of trying to expand the company's model offerings to compete more widely with the GM/Ford/Chrysler triumvirate finally led to cars that self-respecting musclecar enthusiasts could drive. The 1968 AMC Javelin was cut straight from the Mustang-inspired ponycar mold. Its stablemate, the AMX, however, was something entirely different. Not quite true sportscar, not quite ponycar, the two-seater held down its own corner of the market. Engine choices for the two included a 290-ci four-barrel V-8, a 343-ci V-8, and a 390-ci V-8 rated at 315 horsepower.

Late to the party, AMC hoped to make a splash with the Javelin in Trans-Am racing in 1968. It was AMC's first attempt at big-time auto racing, and the company did its best to make a good impression. The Javelins were painted in striking red, white, and blue colors. The pit crews were dressed in matching jackets. AMC signed the talented George Follmer and Peter Revson as team drivers. If nothing else, the Javelin team sure *looked* good.

The Javelins ran AMC's 290-ci V-8 bored out to 304 cubic inches, with the engines initially built by Traco. AMC entered the year with high hopes and substantial funding, but the Javelin team was unable to notch a victory. They did score several second-place finishes that first season, with Follmer taking four seconds, Revson two more.

The situation was even more frustrating in 1969. George Follmer signed with Bud Moore's Mustang team, while Peter Revson jumped to Carroll Shelby's competing Mustang squad. John Martin and Ron Grable replaced them. Unfortunately, continued reliability problems dropped AMC to fourth place in the 1969 manufacturers' championship. Grable was the highest-finishing Javelin driver, ending the season in ninth place in the standings

Despite the corporate attention, the Javelins had teething problems, and did not impress everyone. Mustang pilot Whelan thought that "the AMC's were basically pieces of junk," he said. "They would go through motors, and had chassis problems."

AMC went a long way toward addressing those problems in 1970. The smallest American automaker wrote a very large check to sign the Penske organization to a three-year contract. Besides the professionalism of Roger Penske's team, AMC got drivers Mark Donohue and, again, Peter Revson as team drivers. Although Penske's association with Chevrolet had been successful, resulting in two championships, Chevy was not prepared to match the considerable sum offered by American Motors. AMC wanted to win *bad*.

The 1970 team Javelins continued to be painted in American flag colors, although now they were red, white, and *Sunoco* blue. Reliability improved considerably, with Donohue finishing second at the season-opener at Laguna Seca: The Javelin's long-awaited first victory was earned by Donohue at Bridgehampton in 1970, the fifth race of the season. Donohue won two more that year, but the manufacturer's crown went to Ford, thanks to Parnelli Jones' five wins. With the pitched battle between Jones and Donohue, and the fever-pitch involvement of the automakers, 1970 is usually seen as the zenith of Trans-Am racing. Fortunately, it was not yet the zenith for AMC.

Just winning was huge for AMC, however. For the street, AMC built a special Mark Donohue edition Javelin SST. Its most distinguishing characteristic was its large rear deck spoiler complete with "Mark Donohue" signature. The spoiler was advertised as being designed by Donohue himself, but

Parnelli Jones won the 1970 SCCA Trans-Am manufacturers' championship for Ford behind the wheel of a Boss 302, scoring five wins in 11 races. The series did not offer a drivers' championship until 1971, although Jones is listed as the top points racer for 1970. Mark Donohue drove the Penske Javelin to its best year ever to that point, giving AMC second place in the points race. The 1970 season, considered the most exciting by many, featured several pitched battles between Jones and Donohue. *Bob Tronolone*

more importantly, by putting it on the production car the spoiler was homologated for competition use. The 1970 Mark Donohue Javelin came standard with AMC's 360-ci V-8, rated at 290 horsepower, with a 325-horse 390-ci V-8 optional. AMC also offered a red, white, and blue paint option for the street Javelin lifted straight from the factory race cars.

In 1971 Donohue slaughtered the field en route to the manufacturer's title and the newly instituted driver's championship. Donohue won 7 out of 10 races, including a string of six in a row. George Follmer repeated the feat in 1972, winning four of seven events. But by then the Trans-Am championship carried with it fewer bragging rights than it had only two years earlier. Ford and Chrysler had withdrawn factory support after 1970, and with the big dollars had gone most of the big-name drivers. Beating a bunch of privateers just didn't have the same impact, so AMC ended factory sponsorship of its Trans-Am teams at the end of the 1972 season.

Still, of the American automakers, AMC was especially aggressive in creating advertising that tied the street Javelin to its Trans-Am counterpart. In case anyone missed the connection, one print

ad from 1969 displayed "A Javelin for the track. A Javelin for the road," with a helmet-wearing driver leaning against a race Javelin, while a scarf-wearing everyman posed with his red, white, and blue street Javelin. "From zero to Donohue in 3.1 years," AMC bragged in 1970. One ad from late 1971 pictured Donohue's championship-winning car with a list of its seven victories. A stock 1972 Javelin AMX was pictured in the lower right corner, almost as an afterthought.

AMC's years in the Trans-Am series were the company's high-water mark in racing competition. In later years, Matadors were raced in NASCAR, and Jeeps in kidney-busting desert endurance events, but never again did AMC show the purpose, resolve, and flair it displayed in its Trans-Am effort. The championships were a well-deserved reward for the effort.

New Boss

As the factories funneled more and more money and effort into Trans-Am competition it became nearly impossible for privateers to keep up. And it wasn't just because the factories had good drivers and new equipment. The Ford, Chevy, and AMC teams were ruthless in sidestepping the rules.

Subtle differences between the Mach 1 and the Boss 302 included the elimination of the quarter panel scoops on the Boss. Although the rear deck spoiler and rear window slats were ordered on most 1970 Boss 302 Mustangs, some buyers ordered them without the popular options.

"In 1969 and 1970 it really started getting tough," recalled Mustang privateer Jim Whelan. "In 1970 the really good cars were silhouette cars. They were scaled up," he said. "When they started spending a lot of money on chassis, doing a lot of stuff, the cars didn't look quite right, but the tech inspectors could not figure out why."

Many of the top Mustangs were actually 7/8-scale knock-offs. Much of the sheet metal (and chassis) was acid dipped. "You had to put a substantial roll cage in to keep the car together," Whelan said.

To keep up, everyone else had to bend the rules to the outside limit, even the independents. "The

The Boss 302 V-8 certainly had good visual presence, thanks to the shaker hood scoop option. Although quick, the Boss 302 V-8's large ports and valves ensured the engine was more comfortable in a high-revving race environment than the street. The oil cooler mounted in front of the radiator in this image is part of the optional Drag Pack.

The American Motors team crashed the Trans-Am party in 1968 with team drivers. The Javelins began asserting themselves in 1970, with Mark Donohue earning AMC's first three wins. Donohue's teammate, Peter Revson, is shown here at Laguna Seca in 1970. *Bob Tronolone*

rules were, you had to have doors that opened," Whelan said. "On our car, to open it you had to take a bolt off a pin, and loosen two bolts off the front because it pivoted off the two bolts. It was a gutted shell! But it would open, to meet the rules."

Trans-Am cars were also supposed to be built with factory performance parts, available to the public. But many a "factory" part emerging from Bud Moore's shop arrived with hand-engraved Ford part numbers.

For the Mustang teams in 1969, an even more serious street car with Trans-Am designs had worked its way through the Ford system. Intended to meet the Z28 Camaro head-on, Ford produced a special Mustang with a 302-ci engine that had Trans-Am fingerprints all over it. The main strengths of the "Boss 302," as the new package was called, were cylinder heads with massive ports and valves, perfect for ramming large quantities of air and fuel through the engine at high rpm.

A midyear introduction, Ford had to hustle to build enough Boss 302s to qualify for the season. As the rules stated, "SCCA Sedan Category automobiles shall normally be those which are series-produced with normal road touring equipment in quantities of at least 1,000 within a 12-month period." On

May 5, 1969, the SCCA certified the minimum number of 1,000 Boss 302 Mustangs had been built. Ford wasted no time informing the public about the new Mustang's mission in life. "Nearest thing to a Trans-Am Mustang that you can bolt a license plate onto," print ads boasted in the spring of 1969.

The new engine required new planning and procedures for the Ford teams. Jim Whelan, who had started his Trans-Am career in 1967 with a Shelby-ized 1966 Mustang, made the move to Boss 302 when they became available. He ran a 1969 body-in-white Mach 1 with the Boss 302 engine.

"The Boss 302 engines were very fussy motors," he said. "To get power out of them, you had to run them at huge rpm. They had humongous lift cams—.610, .650 lift. You had to break the motor and the cam in with light valve springs and go through a certain procedure or you'd flatten the cam and a set of lifters instantaneously. They were using umbrella lifters, lifters with a big base. So if something happened, you couldn't just pull the lifters out. You had to pull the cam, and pull the lifters out from the bottom. It was NASCAR technology."

It wasn't just break-in procedure that was serious business. Parts selection was more complicated. "Since dry sumps were illegal, Ford had this wet/dry sump system, which was this crazy oil pump, crazy pan, with all sorts of pick-ups throughout the pan," Whelan said. "They were really exotic."

The racing blocks didn't use traditional head gaskets, using instead stainless steel o-rings, with rubber o-rings for the water passages. "The car would idle at about 3000 rpm," Whelan said. "It would put out power from about 5000 rpm on up. We'd limit ours to 8500 rpm, but the factory guys were running 10,500." Which meant, in turn, they had to be geared to run that rpm. "Once you got them broken in, they were pretty darn reliable. And they put out just gobs of power. They were stronger than anything else out there," Whelan said.

As a race car, Whelan remembers the Boss 302 as being the ride to have. He recalls the Z28 as being solid, but probably not as good as the Mustang. "Chassis-wise, I think the Mustangs were better," he said. "In the factory cars the Mustangs had the power. I think so much with the Camaros was Donohue. He made a very so-so car—along with Penske's preparation—into an almost unbeatable car."

Almost unbeatable certainly described the 1969 season for Donohue. Despite the new Boss 302 Mustang's strengths, Donohue and his Z28 won six races and the manufacturers' championship for Chevrolet (with an assist from Ronnie Bucknum, who also notched a Camaro victory). Parnelli Jones, driving a Grabber Orange Bud Moore Boss, scored two victories and a handful of seconds. In 1970 the drivers swapped position in the standings, as Jones and the maturing Boss 302 were able to squeak out a one-point lead for the championship over the first-year Penske/Donohue Javelin team.

On the street the Boss 302 cut a "look-at-me" profile thanks to generous striping, but some differences were a bit more subtle. For example, the decorative "scoop" was eliminated from the quarter panels. But mostly people noticed the unique C-stripe, the matte black hood, the front chin spoiler,

Luring Roger Penske and Mark Donohue from Chevrolet was a major coup for AMC, and the company parlayed Donohue's fame into a special street model. Putting the special Mark Donohue Javelin's rear spoiler into production allowed the Javelin team to use it in competition. Standard Mark Donohue Javelin engine was the 360-ci V-8; AMC's 390 was optional.

and rear deck spoiler. The Boss 302 was styled by Larry Shinoda, a recent convert from General Motors who had also been responsible for the design of the 1963 Stingray.

Besides the stout engine and bold looks, Ford used the Boss 302 platform to improve the Mustang's handling. In a *Car and Driver* preview test from June 1969, the editors were particularly impressed by the Boss' handling prowess. "But the Boss 302 is another kind of Mustang," they noted. "It simply drives around the turns with a kind of

This prototype of the Dodge Challenger T/A lacks the final version's "340 Six Pack" fender graphics and fat "T/A" stripes, but includes the important production hardware Dodge wanted to use in competition: the fiberglass hood with jutting scoop, rear ducktail spoiler, and side-exit exhaust. *DaimlerChrysler Corporate Historical Collection*

detachment never before experienced in a street car wearing Ford emblems."

"Without a doubt the Boss 302 is the best handling Ford ever to come out of Dearborn and may just be the new standard by which everything from Detroit must be judged."

As for the Boss engine in street trim, well, nobody ever said building a raceable street car wouldn't require a few compromises. The cylinder heads' large ports and valves (later known as the "Cleveland" heads when adapted to the new 351 in 1970) that helped the Trans-Am cars breathe made for a street engine that often didn't like street rpm. The final drive ratio selected played a part in how well the car was suited for the street, but the combination of small displacement and high-winding power band did not always deliver on its potential, particularly when the engine was ordered in the Mercury Cougar Eliminator, a heavyweight by ponycar standards.

The Boss 302 enjoyed a short life. The model returned for 1970, scoring its best sales and the Trans-Am championship. But in a major retrenchment, in November 1970 Ford Motor Company pulled out of all forms of motorsport. Ford had already dramatically cut its racing budget for the 1970 season. The company had spent untold millions on motorsports in the 1960s, but with the new decade priorities had shifted. Emission control and safety regulations were the new goals,

and the cold-turkey pull-out from racing destroyed most of the goodwill and excitement Ford created in the 1960s.

The Boss name survived another year, as the Boss 351 Mustang. Although widely recognized as one of the fastest and best street rides from the waning days of the musclecar era, the Boss 351 never earned a racing legacy of its own, beyond a smattering of drag racing victories. Parnelli Jones' championship in the 1970 Trans-Am season proved to be the high-water mark for racing Mustangs—until a revival in the 1980s.

Late Arrivals

For Chrysler Corporation, the 1970 Trans-Am season represented a second chance of sorts—a do-over in the ponycar wars.

Although the Plymouth Barracuda entered the market at the same time as Ford's Mustang—even beat it to market by a couple weeks—the ungainly little glassback coupe had never matched the huge sales figures posted by the Mustang. Dodge had been left out of the ponycar market altogether, with various Dart, Coronet, and Charger models tasked with the high-performance heavy lifting. Because of these reasons, the new 1970 Barracuda and Dodge Challenger models, and the Trans-Am circuit were a vital part of corporate plans. Based on a new E-body chassis, the Challenger and Barracuda were expected to crack the code on a major section of the youth market. Handsomely styled, the E-body fraternal twins could be ordered with every engine in Chrysler's passenger car line-up, with option packages targeted to nearly every demographic.

The SCCA's Trans-Am series could serve as a major boost to the credibility of the new cars, if done properly. At least, that was the thinking in 1968, with the Mopar E-bodies still under development and the Trans-Am nearing its peak in popularity. When the calendar flipped over to 1970, however, the ponycar market was considerably softer and the Trans-Am was a season away from implosion.

That future was not yet evident as Chrysler readied its new ponycars for 1970. The racing plans proceeded promisingly enough. Popular driver Dan Gurney announced in the fall of 1969 that he had signed a deal with Plymouth for 1970. He would race one car, with a second Barracuda for Swede Savage. His team was named the All American Racers. The Dodge team, fielded by the Autodynamics shop, signed Sam Posey as lead driver.

As Chrysler no longer built a V-8 smaller than 318 cubic inches, the racing E-bodies were powered by destroked 340-ci small-block V-8s, displacing 303 cubic inches. The teams raced special production models festooned with race-inspired hood scoops and spoilers, named the AAR 'Cuda and T/A Challenger.

Despite the corporate push, the racing Challengers and Barracudas carried notable disadvantages into competition. The cars were wide and a bit portly, a side effect of building a production car with an engine bay large enough to accommodate everything from a 225-ci slant six to the 426 Hemi. The Mopars also lagged behind in chassis development.

Those shortcomings manifested themselves immediately. Gurney especially was plagued by mechanical maladies and bad luck. Savage's best finish in 1970 was a second place at Road America. Posey managed three third-place finishes, and ended the season in fourth place, one spot ahead of Savage.

The AAR 'Cuda was Plymouth's attempt to build a Trans-Am car. Its special features included the unique fiberglass hood with scoop. It shared a side-exit exhaust design with the T/A Challenger.

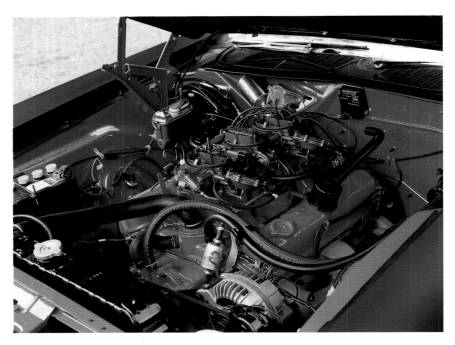

The street version of the AAR 'Cuda sported a 340 Six Pack V-8, an engine exclusive to the special 'Cuda and the Dodge T/A Challenger. The race versions of the AAR 'Cuda used a destroked, single four-barrel-equipped small-block displacing 303 cubic inches to comply with Trans-Am rules. The Six Pack street engine was rated at 290 horsepower; the race engines usually spun the dyno up to 450.

Even though the AAR 'Cudas and T/A Challengers were a day late and a victory short at the track, they made striking street cars. Produced in 1970 only, the two certainly looked as if they were built with racing in mind. Both cars were fitted with side-exit exhaust, an unusual system that featured front-entry, front-exit mufflers. The Challenger came standard with a center-mounted, forward-leaning hood scoop, while the AAR 'Cuda's scoop started near the leading edge of its fiberglass hood and ran toward the back, like some aircraft NACA duct. Both had small deck spoilers, and striking graphics packages.

The standard, and only, engine available was a 340-ci smallblock with the three-two-barrel "Six Pack" induction. It was underrated at, not coincidentally, 290 horsepower, the same as the Boss 302 and Camaro Z28. The 340 Six Pack was offered exclusively in the T/A Challenger and AAR 'Cuda.

Plans were made to continue the two cars for 1971, but Chrysler cut back its own racing program late in 1970, effectively killing the rationale for further production. Dodge already had an R/T Challenger for performance enthusiasts, and Plymouth had a 'Cuda model, making the T/A and AAR expensive redundancies.

The short career of the T/A Challenger and AAR 'Cuda left a mixed legacy. The cars never won in SCCA Trans-Am competition, but the street versions are some of the most sought-after muscle-cars among collectors. The unique engine, impressive performance, and one-year availability make the street duo far more memorable than the factory-supported E-body racers. Had Chrysler stuck with its Trans-Am program, however, the reverse could very well have come true.

The Survivor

Pontiac's entry into Trans-Am racing was both a smashing success and a dismal failure. Successful, in that when the general public hears the name "Trans-Am" today it usually thinks of Pontiac's top-line, high-profile Firebird, not the SCCA's decades-old professional racing series. The Sports Car Club of America may legally own the rights to the name, but as far as most people are concerned, a "Trans-Am" is a hot rod Firebird. For that reason alone it was worth Pontiac's time to get involved in the Trans-Am series.

It certainly didn't look that way in 1969. The Firebird had a tough go in the Trans-Am series. The street Firebird was introduced after the Camaro's debut, and therefore the racing Firebirds did not land in the Trans-Am series until late 1968. The new pony-car had one built-in disadvantage: Pontiac had no V-8 smaller than 326 cubic inches, so the division had to begin a 5-liter engine program if it wanted to race in Trans-Am. While Pontiac's proposed 303-ci V-8 was under development, Firebird racers ran 302-ci Z28 engines, deemed legal because Canadian Pontiacs were fitted with Chevrolet V-8s.

The 303, as proposed, would have been a beast. Although loosely based on the 400-ci Pontiac engine, the 303 used its own special block. The engine's unique feature was its tunnel port cylinder heads, which should have provided excellent breathing characteristics. However, during testing engineers discovered the Ram Air IV heads used on the 400 V-8 actually provided superior performance when mounted on the 303.

The engine was originally planned to debut in a special Firebird model named after the racing series itself, the Trans-Am. The new model was designed with hard-to-miss scoops and spoilers as standard equipment, making them legal for competition. Pontiac paid a $5 royalty per car to the SCCA for use of the name, an economic arrangement that survived for decades.

Unfortunately, the 303 engine program went nowhere. The development time lost on the tunnel port heads delayed the engine's introduction. The 303 did see limited racing duty in 1970, but by then time, and the rule book, had passed by the special Pontiac V-8. Thanks in part to the delay, the production Firebird Trans-Am was released in the spring of 1969 with a 400-ci engine. Pontiac was saddled with the ironic situation of creating a Trans-Am model that, as built from the factory, could not legally run in the series.

Tellingly, the original press release announcing the car, dated March 7, 1969, to coincide with the Chicago Auto Show, made no mention of the SCCA's Trans-Am series or the new Firebird model's connection to it.

At least the Firebird Trans-Am looked like it was ready for the track. All 1969 Trans-Ams were painted white with twin blue racing stripes. Also unique to the model were functional side air extractors, a large fiberglass deck spoiler and hood with two scoops at the leading edge. The base engine was Pontiac's Ram Air 400, rated at 335 horsepower. The Ram Air IV, with its 345 horsepower, was optional.

The AAR acronym stood for All-American Racers, the name of Dan Gurney's race teams from the 1960s into the late 1990s.

The Firebird Trans-Am was introduced at the Chicago Auto show in 1969, along with the GTO Judge. The Judge was more popular that year, but the Trans-Am got the last laugh with 33 years of uninterrupted production. Extroverted rear wing and various scoops and stripes were laughed at when new, but the design looks positively tame compared to what followed in the 1970s. *Pontiac Historic Services*

It may have taken its name from the SCCA's sedan-based series, but Pontiac's early Trans-Am was never a force in actual Trans-Am competition. It was, however, a superior street car, arguably the best of the 1970s musclecars. The 1971 edition, pictured, came standard with a 335-horsepower 455 V-8. As far as handling prowess, the T/A was practically a Formula 1 ride compared to the various "high-performance" Torinos, Novas, and Chargers of the time. The Pontiac Trans-Am eventually redeemed itself in its namesake racing series, with Elliott Forbes-Robinson winning the drivers' and manufacturers' titles in 1982.

Less visible were the Trans-Am's heavy duty springs and shocks, large anti-sway bar, high-effort variable ratio power steering, and high-effort power front disc brakes. Pontiac signature options like the hood-mounted tachometer were also available.

The boy-racer Firebird proved to be an acquired taste though, as only 697 were ever built, most hardtops, but also eight convertibles. Even the press got in a few digs at the Trans-Am. "The decals don't belong here," wrote Steve Kelly in a 1969 *Hot Rod* test of a preproduction Trans-Am. "They just don't cut it in the looks department. If metal script can't be used, it's better to have nothing at all in the lettering department."

two or three best-looking cars to emerge from the musclecar era.

The new Trans-Am sported a body-colored grille/bumper arrangement far removed from the traditional chrome bumper. Air extractors on the fenders returned, although better looking and functional. The hood was dominated by a "shaker" hood scoop that vibrated to the engine's rumblings. The Trans-Am was still white and blue, with a single fat blue stripe running over the top. Inside was a slick engine-turned dash and fat, grippy steering wheel. Although still few in number, production of the Trans-Am improved to 3,196.

Pontiac may have fixed the street Trans-Am, but the Firebird's first SCCA Trans-Am victory didn't come until Milt Mintner took the checkered at Mid Ohio in 1972. The car was essentially a racing nonfactor in the 1960s and 1970s, but patience eventually won the day. In 1982 the Pontiac Trans-Am finally won the championship in its namesake racing series.

This lack of stature at the race track proved to be no impediment to the Trans-Am's long-term viability, however. The Trans-Am was hugely popular in the mid- to late 1970s, just as the racing series was cratering, with production increasing continuously between 1972 and 1979. In the peak year, 1979, Pontiac built 117,109 Trans-Ams, representing more than half of all Firebird production. The Trans-Am's popularity resulted partly from the car being one of the very few 1970s-era performance cars with real cubic inches and real muscle. As late as 1976 the Trans-Am could be ordered with a 455-ci V-8. The other factor in the Trans-Am's popularity was its wild styling, complete with fender flares, shaker hood scoop, and infamous "screaming chicken" hood decal. The car became a pop icon, eventually becoming more famous than the series that spawned its name.

Of all the specialty musclecars that resulted from the auto manufacturers attempts to dominate the SCCA's Trans-Am racing series, the most popular at the time was the 1969 Z28 Camaro. It reached production of 20,302 in 1969, a number substantially higher than in any year of Boss 302, Donohue Javelin, AAR 'Cuda, or T/A Challenger production.

Long term, however, the Pontiac Firebird Trans-Am has been the most enduring survivor of the series. It has been in continuous production from 1969 to 2001, the only musclecar model originating in the 1960s that can lay such a claim. It's only fitting that the longest-lived car influenced by the Trans-Am series should be the one that adopted its name.

On the track, T/G Racing, with Jerry Titus as lead driver, was the most prominent Firebird team. Despite the delays and setbacks, Titus drove his Firebird to third in the points standings for 1969, although victory lane remained beyond reach. Milt Mintner also helped in securing Pontiac's third-place finish in the manufacturers' championship.

The Firebird Trans-Am returned for 1970, and at least that particular year earned more respect on the street, if not on the track. Thanks to a dramatic restyling and substantial suspension improvements, the car earned lavish praise from the automotive press. The 1970 Trans-Am was arguably one of the

PACE CARS

As the granddaddy of American auto races for most of the twentienth century, the Indianapolis 500 has always had an outsized presence in the automotive universe. Sure, the Daytona 500 is big, and various races at Talladega, Charlotte, Watkins Glen, and Long Beach have garnered prestige and large numbers of fans, but Indy has been an event unto itself. Some years it almost seemed as if the rest of the Indy Car races on the schedule were an afterthought.

Obviously, musclecars from the glory days of the 1960s and early 1970s did not race at the track, yet just leading the race cars around the famed Brickyard was considered so prestigious that manufacturers readily spent millions to provide vehicles for pace car duty. They also spun off pace car replicas (or slightly used festival cars) to sell alongside their standard offerings, and some of these were pretty special in their own right.

(Some definitions: "Actual pace cars" refers to the one or two, sometimes three, vehicles specially modified to lead the cars around the track before the race and during caution periods. These were usually heavily massaged for their high-speed duty. "Festival cars" refers to the dozens of look-alike cars provided for use by track officials and VIPs in the days leading up to the race. These cars were often sold through local dealerships after the race. "Pace car replicas" are the commemorative models sold to the general public by the manufacturers, which are usually, but not always,

Ford's Mustang has been selected as the Indianapolis 500 pace car three times—1964, 1979, and 1994. Each time was in a year when the Mustang had been substantially redesigned.

Everything else went right for the Mustang in 1964, so why not pace Indy? The pace cars had a special white paint with single blue stripe, and blue dashboards.

straight production-line vehicles sold with "Official Pace Car" graphics.)

Getting picked to provide Indy pace cars is not a simple selection process. Any manufacturer making a bid to supply Indy pace cars also coughs up dozens of festival cars, VIP cars, sometimes even trucks and emergency vehicles. It's a major commitment, although also a publicity bonanza. The Big Three pick and choose their spots carefully, trying to coordinate a pace car bid with the introduction of an important new model. And, at least so far, the pace car plum has been one reserved for American manufacturers.

Ford Must Race

Each time the Mustang served as the Indy pace car—1964, 1979, 1994—it was at a major junction in the car's life, usually a turn for the better. At the traditional Memorial Day race in 1964 the Mustang was brand new, only a couple months removed from its public introduction, and still the object of frenzied desire. In 1979 the Mustang was shaking off the forgettable Mustang II years with a crisply designed new body and modern Fox chassis.

And in 1994 that same (by then creaky and old) Fox chassis and the remnants of the original 1979 design were laid to rest as yet another stylish new Mustang was introduced.

There have been other reasons for Ford to be at Indy. The company, teamed with Cosworth Engineering, has usually been an engine supplier for the series. The job of leading the pack at Indy has also served as another forum for the endless Mustang vs. Camaro war. As for drivers, Ford has managed to keep the pace car driver's seat in the family. In 1964 and 1966 (in a Mercury Cyclone GT), Benson Ford was the pace car driver; in 1968 (the Torino GT's year) the job went to William C. Ford. In 1979 Jackie Stewart, the former F1 world champion who has long worked as a consultant for Ford, drove the pacer. The 1994 pacing duties went to Parnelli Jones, a winner of the 1963 Indy 500, but also the 1970 SCCA Trans-Am champion while driving a Boss 302 Mustang.

Like everything else associated with the Mustang, the marketing angle for the first Mustang pace cars was played to the hilt. Ford even gave its blessing to a run of toy pedal cars resembling the

Mustang pace cars, which were distributed to the Indy 500 festival committee. For grown-ups, Ford established a "checkered flag" contest, in which its top-selling dealers won pace car replica hardtop Mustangs, along with a free trip to Dearborn to pick up the cars. The 1964-1/2 dealer-contest Mustangs were painted a unique Pace Car White, with a blue racing stripe. They had white interiors and blue dashboards. All were optioned with the 260-ci V-8 and automatic transmissions. Often these Mustangs were left in dealer showrooms to build traffic, but the Indy graphics were painted over before being sold.

The 33 festival cars that were used at the track were slightly different from the contest cars. They were convertibles, painted Wimbledon White, with 289-ci engines and had either manual or automatic transmissions, since they were largely rounded up from dealer stocks.

Ford Motor Company lost interest in racing during the 1970s, but 15 years after the first Mustang paced Indy the Mustang was back. Ford was eager to promote its newest Mustang. The 1979 edition was a clear departure from the Mustangs of the previous 10 years. It was cleanly styled, with an international air about it. It was spacious, yet light of weight. The Mustang's new suspension was tuned to maximize the performance of the special Michelin TRX tires. It had a V-8 engine underhood, but also an optional turbocharged four-cylinder.

The replicas sold for the street were all hatchbacks, painted silver with black-and-red accents. As with many pace car replicas, the "Official Pace Car" decals were not applied at the factory. Ford left

Days before the 1965 Indianapolis 500, veteran driver Don Branson gives rookie driver Mickey Rupp a familiarization ride around the track in a Sport Fury pace car. Steward Paul Johnson is at left. Driver of the pace car on race day was Plymouth general manager P. N. Buckminster. *DaimlerChrysler Corporate Historical Collection*

The 100 or so 1967 Camaro Indy pace cars sold were all used festival cars, not a special model. They were all white and blue SS/RS models.

them loose underneath the hatch, allowing the owner to decide just how flamboyant the Mustang should be. The track car got a special Jack Roush-built smallblock, while the street replicas made do with either the 140-horsepower, two-barrel 302 V-8, or Ford's new turbocharged, 2.3-liter four-cylinder. The 1979 editions were easily the most popular Mustang pace cars, with roughly 11,000 built.

The 1994 Mustang pace car replicas, however, were the most capable. Based on the Cobra model, the 1994 pace car replicas had a 240-horsepower 5.0-liter (302-ci) V-8 underhood. With that kind of firepower, the modifications required for the track cars were minimal. Ford SVT added a roll bar, fuel cell, and a few suspension modifications, and replaced the stock five-speed manual with a specially calibrated automatic.

The 1,000 replicas were all Rio Red convertibles with Saddle Tan interiors and Indy logos on the seat backs. As with the 1979 models, the "Official Pace Car" graphics were supplied in the trunk in case the owner preferred a more low-key ride.

The Mustang wasn't the only Ford to pace Indy, just the most visible. The Thunderbird handled the duty in 1961. Ford's intermediate-size cars also were selected in 1966 and 1968. In 1966 the Mercury Comet nameplate was moved from the compact Falcon chassis to a mid-size platform, and Mercury provided a fleet of Comet Cyclone GT convertibles. "Indy 500 discovers Mercury Cyclone GT!" the division bragged in its print advertising.

Two years later when Ford's intermediates were restyled, the 1968 Torino got its turn. The actual pace cars were noteworthy in that they used Ford's new 428 Cobra Jet engine. The festival cars sold after the race got by with lesser engines, although information on these rare pace cars is limited.

Mopar, Too

Chrysler Corporation has not enjoyed the high profile at Indy that Ford and GM have. Unlike Ford, Chevrolet, Buick, and Oldsmobile (all of which have created powerplants for CART and IRL), Chrysler has not supplied engines for the open-wheel ranks. However, Chrysler *has* tried its hand at the pace car sweepstakes on occasion.

During the musclecar era, the first and most notable pace car from Chrysler was the 1963 300 convertible. These blue convertibles were powered by the company's formidable 413 engine. The 1965 Plymouth Sport Fury pace cars could be ordered with the wedge-head, RB-series big-block 426, rated at 365 horsepower. Plymouth was more aggressive in advertising these cars than earlier pace cars.

In 1971, an Indianapolis area Dodge dealer supplied Indianapolis Motor Speedway with a small fleet of Hemi Orange Challenger convertibles. Since they were not official pace cars, no replicas were sold to the public. However, the festival cars for the 500 which were fitted with a variety of engines and later sold regionally.

It was a long drought for Chrysler before the LeBaron convertible served as pace car in 1987—an event noteworthy more for Carroll Shelby driving the pace car than any production-line spin-off. Part of what kept Chrysler away during the intervening years was the financial turmoil the company suffered during the late 1970s. After Chrysler returned to financial health, however, the company had few products suitable for the task, having shifted nearly all of it product line to front-wheel-drive and four-cylinder engines in the early 1980s. A Plymouth Reliant pace car would have been as out of place as, well, a K-car on a race track.

The 1990s have been a different story entirely. Chrysler, flush with cash and conducting business with a confident swagger, built two of the most desirable pace cars ever. The V-10-powered Dodge Viper was first seen as a 1989 concept car. It proved so popular that Chrysler scheduled it for production with a 1992 model-year debut. The buzz surrounding the car was so great, though, that Dodge rushed out a preproduction Viper RT/10 for the 1991 Indy 500. Since the Dodge design team had been inspired by Carroll Shelby's Cobras (and Shelby had been aligned with Dodge since the early 1980s—see chapter 6), Shelby himself drove the pace car.

That first Viper had been the no-frills, topless RT/10, but the car's next evolution proved reason enough for Dodge to sign up again. The 1996 Viper GTS was the new coupe model, possessing a stunning shape that made Chevrolet's Corvette look like a rental car by comparison. With 450 horsepower on tap, the Viper GTS needed little massaging to pull pace car duty. The package was so successful, Dodge produced a run of Indy 500 Special Edition Ram pickups painted in the Viper's blue and white colors.

Camaros and Corvettes

The Chevrolet Camaro and Corvette have been Indy pace car stalwarts, selected 4 times each since 1967. The pace car replicas they spawned are among the more collectible examples of the breed.

The Camaro's first appearance was in the car's debut year, 1967. Although bidding to make Chevrolet's new entry in the ponycar market a pace car seems like a no-brainer, it was problematic because General Motors still had its corporate policy against factory-sponsored racing and racing-oriented marketing. When Chevrolet's bid was accepted for 1967, GM hadn't had one of its products lead the pack at Indy since 1960, when the job went to the Oldsmobile Ninety-Eight. Chevrolet hadn't been the pace leader since 1955. That was a considerable gap in time for the world's largest automaker and its top-selling division to be away from the world's single largest auto race.

Despite the obvious questions a Camaro Indy pace car raised about GM's commitment to

For 1969 Chevrolet sold Indy pace car replicas, not just the used festival cars. All were white convertibles with Hugger Orange stripes and orange houndstooth interiors.

The 1970 Oldsmobile 442 Indy pace car was one of the more attractive musclecars to lead the pack. The pace car package could be ordered on either the Cutlass or 442. *Mike Mueller archives*

a no-racing policy, the corporation rationalized away the inconsistency by maintaining the whole exercise was merely about publicity and exposure for the new product.

The 1967 Indy pace cars sold to the public were not limited edition replicas; rather, they were the 100 or so festival cars built for track officials, and later sold used through area Chevrolet dealers. All 1967 pace cars were white SS/RS models with blue interiors. The festival cars were delivered with the full range of SS engine options, including at least a few with the 375-horsepower L78 396.

Chevrolet was better prepared to exploit the marketing possibilities the next time around. For 1969, Chevrolet built actual pace car replicas to be sold throughout the dealer network. The 3,675 Super Sport convertibles built were white with Hugger Orange stripes, and orange houndstooth interiors. Most were shipped to dealers on the East and West

coasts, where weather was better suited for convertibles. Later in the year, to placate Midwest dealers, Chevrolet created an unknown number of so-called Z-10 Camaro coupes. These cars, based on the SS, had the Hugger Orange-over-white stripes of the convertibles, but no Indy graphics.

Going by absolute numbers, the 1982 Z28 Indy pace car was either the most popular of the Camaro pace cars or simply the least exclusive. It was sold as a separate model, not just an option, and Chevrolet built 6,360 of them. Measured in terms of pure acceleration the 1982 model was the weakest of the four Camaro pace cars, although in a handling contest the 1982 would have left earlier Camaros sitting in melting pools of bias-ply rubber.

The color scheme for 1982 was silver and blue with red stripes. That year the top engine for the street replicas was the 305 V-8, with either single four-barrel and 145 horsepower, or "Cross Fire

Injection" with dual throttle bodies and 165 horsepower, but with automatic transmission only.

For the track, the two actual pace cars were fitted with 350-ci engines with aluminum heads, forged pistons, headers, and an 11.0:1 compression ratio—in short, exactly the powertrain Camaro lovers were hoping would be available for order in the new Z28, but had been rendered impossible to produce thanks to strict emission control and corporate average fuel economy requirements.

Fortunately, by the time the 1993 Camaro pace cars came into being, the magic of computer control and electronic fuel injection had allowed for both good power and respectable fuel economy. The stock 1993 Z28's 5.7-liter V-8 was rated at 275 horsepower. Needless to say, the 1993 Z28 pace car required far less tweaking than the 1980s version to perform its duties on the track. The 1993 models also recaptured the missing air of exclusivity—only 633 were built.

The Corvette has always been a hybrid, a sports cars with a musclecar engine. Surprisingly, considering the Corvette's position as the country's premier sports car, 25 years passed from the time of the Corvette's introduction in 1953 to its first tour of Indy pace car duty. The first Indy pace car Corvettes arrived in 1978, as part of the 'Vette's 25th anniversary year. The attractive black and silver pace car replicas were hugely popular, with production of 6,502.

In 1986 the Corvette had another milestone to celebrate, the return of the roadster, off the market

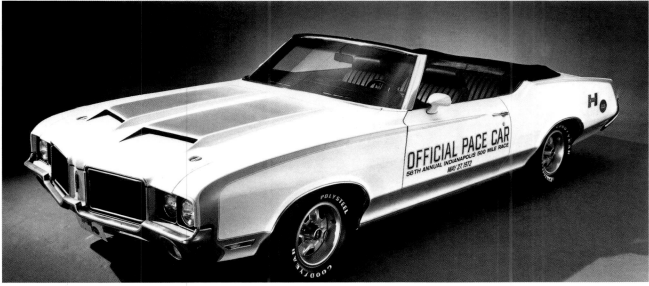

Hurst was the sole supplier of the 1972 Indy pace cars, not Oldsmobile. The pace cars came with low-compression 455 V-8s, but were bolstered with 1970-spec W-30 engine parts. *Olds History Center*

since 1975. The pace car replicas were hard to miss in their bright yellow paint. The 1995 and 1998 Corvette pace car replicas brought startling horsepower, the latter 345, to the track, numbers reminiscent of the horsepower wars of the 1960s.

442 at the 500

Oldsmobile had a strong presence at Indy during the 1970s, producing some of the best pace car replicas of the era. They didn't do it alone. The division had an important partner of sorts in Hurst Performance, manufacturer of popular Hurst shifters, wheels, and accessories. The company had a respected reputation among performance enthusiasts, and, if nothing else, Hurst knew the ins and outs of promotion.

Hurst was not around for the 1970 pace car, though. After 10 years on the sidelines, Oldsmobile threw its corporate hat into gasoline alley that year. The 442 could be ordered with Oldsmobile's big 455 V-8 for the first time, and the W30, rated at 370 horsepower, was the top performance version. The pace cars were white 442 convertibles with red and black lettering.

The softening of the musclecar market in the early 1970s resulted in a noticeable lack of enthusiasm from Detroit for the whole pace car extravaganza. It was a great opportunity for a small manufacturer to make inroads, so Hurst went out on its own in bidding for the 1972 pace car business. The 1972 Hurst/Olds Indy pace cars and festival cars were provided entirely by Hurst.

The actual pace cars that year ran with 455-ci V-8s upgraded with 1970 W-30 heads and cam, and the W-30-spec torque converter. The white and gold festival cars Hurst provided and later sold were a mixed bag of Hurst Cutlass hardtops and convertibles. In *The Hurst Heritage*, a thorough history of the marque published in 1986, authors Robert Lichty and Terry Boyce report Hurst even supplied six H/O station wagons and a lone sedan for Indy use.

Oldsmobile and Hurst returned to the track a mere two years later. The Cutlass had been given an odd-looking restyle for 1973, but Oldsmobile's intermediate was proving increasingly popular. The pace cars for 1974 ranged much further from stock specs than many previous pace cars. The two actual track cars had the roofs removed and replaced with special targa bars. The H/O replicas did without the open-air feature, although they had special roof bands that mimicked the look. Based on the Cutlass S, the pace car replicas could be ordered with either a 180-horsepower 350 V-8, or 250-horse W30 455 V-8. Hurst also produced a run of Indy Delta 88 convertibles for festival and parade car use.

This Mach 1 was one of American Raceways Inc.'s pace car Mustangs from Texas International Speedway. Each of the Corporation's tracks got their own color Mustang. With its 351 Cleveland V-8 underhood, this Mustang was likely used for parade duty. Actual pace cars generally had the 428 CJ.

Still an Indy pace car, although a different sort entirely. Opponents maintained the world would explode if any race other than the Memorial Day classic was held at the track, yet the Brickyard seems to have survived its brush with NASCAR with no harm done. The annual Brickyard 400 even has its own pace car; in 1997 it was a 30th anniversary Camaro.

Away from Indy

The Indianapolis Motor Speedway may have been the kingmaker when it came to pace cars, but it wasn't the only track in America that needed something to lead packs of snarling race cars to the green flag. In the late 1960s and early 1970s one of America's important motorsport corporations was American Raceways Inc. The company owned several prominent race tracks coast to coast. American Raceways tried to tie their tracks together by using similar logos, and, for a while, similar pace cars.

At the peak, in 1970, American Raceways teamed with Ford for a collection of unique Mach 1 Mustang pace cars. Ford even went so far as to place advertising in racing programs around the country. "It takes a great car to set the pace on the five great tracks of American Raceways, Inc.— Michigan International, Riverside, Atlanta, Texas International and Eastern International," the ads crowed. "And Mustang paces them all. Because Mustang's a mover."

All the American Raceways Mach 1s carried the unique American Raceways logos on the quarter panels, with a stylized letter-shaped race track surrounded by the track name. Track cars usually came with the 428 Cobra Jet, although some parade cars were built with the Mach 1s standard 351 V-8.

What about America's other Super Bowl race, NASCAR's Daytona 500? Daytona 500 pace cars have become collectible in their own right, although the cars were traditionally sold only regionally, and had no national marketing campaign behind them. Often a Daytona 500 pace car was the product of an enterprising regional dealership. Pontiac and Daytona have had a particularly close relationship through the years, resulting in such notable Daytona 500 pace cars as the 1967 Firebird, and the 301-ci turbo Trans-Am of 1981.

In modern times, as NASCAR's popularity has grown and the stock cars have staked their own claim on Indy, the Brickyard 400 pace cars have attracted the notice of collectors. A Camaro set the pace in 1997, and the copycat festival cars attracted plenty of attention. If the split between open-wheel sanctioning bodies that erupted in 1996 continues, the term "Indy pace car" may come to have a very different meaning.

CHAPTER
FIVE

DEALER AND MANUFACTURER SPECIALS

With such a wide variety of musclecars available during the 1960s, it's hard to imagine people not being able to find something to satisfy that itch for speed. But mass-produced automobiles are always products of compromise. Engines aren't tuned for maximum power because they have to be able to idle in traffic and run on rotgut gasoline. The largest engine a manufacturer produces may not be put in the company's smallest, sportiest car because the perceived market for such a beast is too small. The absolute fattest tires and priciest wheels are left out of the catalog because regular working people have to be able to afford the car in the first place.

And so, for the serious horsepower junkie, there were indeed many gaps in the 1960s musclecar product line; many niches needed to be explored. Opportunities to fix product deficiencies and to maximize performance arose. Some companies prospered by simply providing cars that were different from what everyone else was driving.

In hindsight, some opportunities in the specialty musclecar field were obvious. Ford's Mustang was wildly popular during its first couple of years, but was hardly a musclecar in the traditional sense. The Corvette's hot 427 was not available in the Nova or Camaro through regular channels, leaving an opening for enterprising dealers. General Motors'

The first GT-350s blew out of Carroll Shelby's California assembly plant more race car than street machine. The 1965 models were delivered with side-exit exhaust, Detroit Locker rear ends, and competition seat belts. You wanted air conditioning, automatic transmission, and a backseat? Ford offered plenty of six-cylinder, whitewall-tired Mustangs for the less stout of heart.

97

Shelby took the stock 271-horsepower Hi-Po 289 and massaged it up to 306 horsepower through the use of Tri-Y headers, an aluminum high-rise intake, and a 715 cfm four-barrel carburetor. Many of Shelby's accessories, such as the finned Cobra valve covers, became Ford high-performance staples. For a time, the small manufacturer overshadowed the larger corporate parent, at least in the performance image department.

intermediate-sized cars were limited by the corporation to 400 cubic inches of displacement until 1970, offering another opportunity.

Attacking these perceived deficiencies were an army of small manufacturers and large auto dealers. The auto dealers usually parlayed their purchasing clout and regional fame into special arrangements with the Big Three that resulted in musclecars that could not be obtained through the usual channels. As for the small manufacturers, they usually had their own separate facilities, and worked closely with the corporate offices to obtain stripped-down production vehicles that could then be rebuilt as limited-production musclecars with their own distinct personalities.

Shelby

Building a car with your name on its flanks is beyond the reach of most mortals, but some people can transfer fame or notoriety into their own car line. Carroll Shelby was one such person.

When Shelby approached Ford in 1961 about the company supplying engines for his proposed sports car project, he carried a lot of credibility into the corporate boardrooms. As a racing driver, he and co-driver Roy Salvadori had won the 24 Hours of Le-Mans sports car race in 1959, and Shelby had won three American sports car championships. He was also a businessman, with a Goodyear tire dealership to his credit.

Shelby's idea involved taking English-made AC Ace sports cars and fitting them with modified versions of Ford's new lightweight small-block V-8. This approach had several advantages for Shelby, not the least of which was minimal manufacturing costs. It was a "best of both worlds" scenario that mated an attractive British sports car body to a powerful, yet reliable, American V-8.

The creation of the Shelby Cobra began a partnership between Carroll Shelby and Ford Motor Company that lasted the rest of the decade. The Cobra's fame far exceeded its sales, but the association with Shelby was an important part of Ford's "Total Performance" campaign. From an image standpoint, the Cobra was pure gravy for Ford.

When the Mustang debuted in 1964 it had few deficiencies as far as the general public was concerned. It was cute, cheap, and sporty enough to project a youthful image. It had that rare appeal that cut across traditional demographic boundaries. As a performance car, however, it was more looker than Saturday night warrior. The Mustang's top engine was a 271-horsepower 289-ci V-8, and its sportiest option was the modest GT package. The performance market was shifting toward cars like the new Pontiac GTO, with its 335-horse Tri-Power 389 V-8. Bigger, more powerful engines were what 1960s car culture demanded. Also, if the Mustang was to be competitive in any type of racing event it needed help.

It was for this reason Ford Motor Company proposed a special Shelby Mustang. Carroll Shelby, despite a full plate of Cobra production and racing commitments, knew a high-profile opportunity when he saw one, and signed on.

Production began at Shelby's Venice, California, plant in 1965. Initially, Shelby built two types of "GT-350" Mustangs, a race version and a street version, although the street version was about as close to a race car as could be driven down main street. The

Carroll Shelby's Mustangs earned their racing reputations at road course events. Shelby successfully ran team cars in SCCA A-Sedan and later in Trans-Am. The cars still compete in vintage racing events; the trio pictured is carving up Sears Point raceway at the 1995 Cobra reunion.

1965 Shelbys were sold with competition seat belts but without rear seats, and all came with a track-ready Detroit Locker rear end. Most 1965 models were sold with loud, side-exiting exhaust.

Shelby started with white, partially complete Mustangs shipped from Ford. The Mustangs came with the 271-horse 289, T-10 four-speed, the Detroit Locker rear end, and larger station wagon rear drum brakes. Shelby modifications to the engine included an aluminum high-rise intake manifold, 715 cfm carburetor, "Tri-Y" headers, and a high-capacity, finned aluminum oil pan, plus dress-up items. The Shelby 289 was rated at 306 horsepower.

To improve handling, the Shelby Mustangs came with an altered front-end geometry, Koni shocks, a one-inch front anti-sway bar, a shock tower brace, and traction bars. Options included 15x6-inch Cragar wheels.

The GT-350R model went even further. The usual weight-reduction strategies were employed, such as a fiberglass hood and front valence, an aluminum panel to replace the quarter window, removal of the carpet and glove box, and the deletion of the rear bumper. Race tuning pushed the engine to roughly 350 horsepower.

The Shelby GT-350's improved performance and hard-to-miss exterior certainly raised the Mustang's performance image, but its high cost and cranky street nature limited the Shelby Mustang's appeal. Consequently, the Shelby Mustangs were toned down for 1966. The rear seat went back in, and the Detroit Locker rear end was made an option. Buyers could order an automatic transmission and air conditioning, luxuries not available in 1965. To further expand the Shelby Mustang's appeal, Shelby produced a run of GT-350H Mustangs available for rent at Hertz.

By 1968 the Shelby Mustang was far removed from its 1965 origins. It was less rough-and-tumble and more oriented toward luxury. The torquey 428 Cobra Jet engine represented a major shift in personality from the high revving 289 of the first Shelby Mustangs. The GT-500KR was the new model that year, as was the convertible body style, but the cars were no longer built at Shelby's California facility.

When Ford restyled and enlarged the Mustang for 1967 it opened up possibilities for Shelby. The car's wider flanks created room for Ford's FE-series big-block V-8. The top regular production option for the Mustang GT was the 390-ci V-8, but as far as physical dimensions go, there was no outward difference between the 390 and the 427 or 428. Shelby took Ford's Police Interceptor 428, rated at 355 horsepower thanks to dual four-barrel carburetors, and dropped it in the Mustang. The result was named the GT-500.

The big-block Shelby Mustangs had different personalities from the earlier road racing-inspired Shelbys. With torquier engines, smoother rides, and less emphasis on turning corners, the GT-500s were more in line with typical musclecars like the Pontiac GTO, Plymouth GTX, and SS396 Chevelle. It was a popular move, as the GT-500 immediately outsold the small-block GT-350.

However, by 1968 the Shelby Mustangs had already begun to lose some of their luster. Sales remained strong, the best ever in fact, but you didn't have to go through Shelby to get a 428 Mustang anymore because Ford released the 428 Cobra Jet option for the GT midway through the 1968 model year. Additionally, the 289-ci V-8's replacement, the 302, was less potent, rated at only 250 horsepower, leaving the GT-350 with more looks than performance. Plus, production and supply issues prompted Ford to push for Shelby Mustang construction to move to Michigan rather than Shelby's California plant.

The 1968 Hurst/Olds, the first of the line, was given a silver and black color scheme. Engine choices consisted of either the W45 or W46 455 V-8. Both were rated at 390 horsepower, although the W46 V-8, destined for air-conditioned cars, was slightly milder. Hurst built 459 two-door hardtops, and 56 Sport coupes for 1968.

Also in 1968, the 428 Police Interceptor V-8 was replaced by the potent single-four-barrel 428 Cobra Jet. But the resulting GT-500 "KR" may have been a bit over the top. In a 1968 GT-500KR road test in *Hot Rod*, Steve Kelly noted, "The KR designation, besides signifying a Cobra Jet-equipped car, reportedly means 'King of the Road.' We decided against further telling of this during our use of either test KR after the first reply to the 'What's the KR mean?' question evoked incredulous laughter. Evidently, the young set isn't ready for that title yet."

The two Shelby Mustangs returned for 1969 and 1970, but with increased musclecar competition from within Ford. In 1969 alone Ford offered a Mustang GT, a Boss 302, a Boss 429, and a Mach 1. That, along with Carroll Shelby's lack of enthusiasm for continued dealings with Ford's bureaucracy, plus

trepidation about upcoming safety and emission regulations, led to the decision by both parties to end Shelby Mustang production. The final 1970 Shelbys were merely retitled and restriped 1969 models. They reflected very little direct Shelby involvement.

But the Shelby Mustangs had done their jobs in 1965 and 1966, giving the Mustang a performance image and giving enthusiasts a car they could purchase without regret. The Cobra name, which Ford purchased from Shelby, continues to signify the top performance Mustang to this very day.

Hurst/Olds

While Carroll Shelby was establishing himself as a respected race car driver, other would-be movers and shakers, such as George Hurst, were trying to secure their own spot in the world of fast automobiles.

One of the classic musclecar ads from the 1960s. With the 1969 Hurst/Olds' twin hood scoops, deck spoiler, 455 V-8, and gold and white paint, there was no sense in running tame advertising.

Born in 1927, Hurst served in the Navy before opening his own auto repair shop in Philadelphia. Hurst's interests branched out to include custom parts such as motor mounts for engine swap conversions and other accessories, but he built his fortune on the popularity of his high-performance shifters. Hurst shifters offered precise gates and short throws, as well as the toughness to withstand the abuse of racing. With partner Bill Campbell, Hurst formed parent company Hurst-Campbell in 1958, with the Hurst Performance Products division pushing the hot rod parts.

The Yenko sYc Camaro is probably the best-known of the high-performance COPO cars. It teamed Chevrolet's biggest, baddest engine, the 427, with the Camaro, which came with no more than 396 cubic inches through regular channels.

The Yenko sYc Camaro came standard with the L72 427, rated at 450 horsepower. The special Camaros came standard with the cowl induction hood. Yenko Chevrolet installed the headers.

Hurst dived headlong into racing. In 1961 Hurst prepared a special Pontiac Catalina to be given away as a prize at the NHRA Nationals, and later in the season a Ford Thunderbird. In 1962 the company built a grand prize Grand Prix to give away at the Nationals. He later sponsored such outrageous exhibition cars as the "Hemi Under Glass" rear-engined Barracuda, and the Hurst Hairy Olds, a Cutlass powered by two 425-ci V-8s. George Hurst was nothing if not a great promoter.

The tremendous street credibility of the Hurst shifters tempted Detroit. Hoping to get a little of the Hurst image to rub off on their performance cars, the automakers one by one signed up Hurst as an Original Equipment Manufacturer (OEM) of shifters. Pontiac was an early believer. The division offered the Hurst shifter as standard equipment on the 1964 GTO. Plymouth jumped in at about the same time, making the Hurst the standard shifter on four-speed-equipped 1964 Plymouth Barracudas.

Later, a whole host of Mopars could be ordered with the shifters, spawning such notables as the "pistol grip." Oldsmobile signed on in 1968, and Buick in 1970 with their GSX. Ford didn't offer the Hurst shifter until 1970. Chevrolet, married to Muncy, was also a latecomer to the Hurst side, but eventually made the sturdy shifters available in their performance cars.

In 1965 Hurst expanded his business into custom wheel sales. The attractive wheels nearly became factory options at Pontiac, although the weight and cost of the wheels eventually disqualified them from production-car status. In 1967 Hurst introduced the dual-gate shifter for automatic transmissions, exposing a whole new segment of the population to the company's wares.

With Hurst products securing their place as part of the hot rodding mainstream, the next step for the company was to branch out into the production of limited edition, specialty musclecars. The best known of these was the Hurst/Olds, a car that immediately raised the performance profile of Oldsmobile's Cutlass line.

Until 1968, the fastest Cutlass was the 442, a car that began life as a hastily contrived competitor for the Pontiac GTO. In many ways the 442 was a more capable car than the GTO. From the beginning, it came with such features as a rear anti-sway bar. But from a sales perspective, the early 442s never caught on. Their styling was conservative to the point of invisibility. The little Olds lived in the shadow of its more popular GM cousins, the GTO and the Malibu SS.

The 442 also had a problem when compared to rivals from other automakers. Ever concerned about projecting an image of irresponsibility, GM policy set limits on power-to-weight ratios that kept engine displacements capped at 400 cubic inches for their intermediate-sized cars (the Olds Cutlass, Pontiac Tempest, Chevrolet Malibu, and Buick Skylark). Other carmakers had no such qualms. In 1968 buyers could equip their Dodge Chargers and Plymouth GTXs with 440 wedge or 426 Hemi V-8s. Ford had a new 428 Cobra Jet option for the Mustang and Torino, which could also be ordered in the Mercury Cyclone. Plus, Oldsmobile had failed to convince GM management to give it a version of the new Camaro/Firebird, a car that could potentially have raised Oldsmobile's profile among youthful buyers.

It was in this environment Hurst found its opportunity for a unique production car. Oldsmobile was a relatively easy sale on the concept of a special edition Cutlass. Hurst quickly lined up production facilities in Lansing, Michigan, through John Demmer, and the Hurst/Olds became a reality in late 1968.

Oldsmobile shipped the Cutlasses—minus the engines—to Lansing. Once there, Hurst dropped in a warmed-over version of Oldsmobile's largest engine, the 455. The Hurst/Olds was the first more-or-less production-based GM intermediate to get a 455 underhood. The 455 was fitted with a high-lift, long-duration cam, Oldsmobile's "Force Air" induction system, and a recurved distributor. The four-barrel carburetor was rejetted for better performance. The top regular production 1968 442 engine was the 400-ci W-30, rated at 360 horsepower and 440 ft-lbs of torque. The 1968 Hurst/Olds brought 390 horsepower, and 500 ft-lbs of torque to the table. With standard 3.91:1 gear ratio, the Hurst/Olds produced ferocious low-end thrust.

According to *The Hurst Heritage,* by Robert Lichty and Terry Boyce, all the 1968 Hurst Oldsmobiles came with TurboHydramatic 400 automatic transmissions and Hurst dual-gate shifters, except for the first car, which was built with a four-speed and used extensively in magazine tests. The cars also came with a full Oldsmobile warranty. All were painted in a Peruvian Silver and black color scheme, although on later cars gold would become the identifying color for Hurst special editions.

Hot Rod magazine, upon testing the 1968 Hurst/Olds, remarked, "Despite the abundance of cubic inches under the louvered hood, emphasis on handling ability is the car's greatest virtue." In actuality, Hurst modifications to the suspension were modest, but the Goodyear G70x14 Polyglas tires helped.

The 1968 Hurst/Olds proved so popular that a 1969 edition was planned immediately. Hurst vehicles were never known for subtlety, but the 1969 Hurst/Olds was especially flamboyant. Painted white with gold striping, the exterior was dominated by two large hood scoops with "H/O 455" emblazoned on the sides, a rear deck spoiler, and European racing mirrors. On the inside, unique gold-striped headrests matched the exterior trim. Tires were upgraded to F60x15, although the 455 was downrated to 380 horsepower. Two Hurst/Olds convertibles were built that year, and used heavily for promotional purposes.

In 1970 the automotive landscape shifted enough to keep a Hurst/Olds out of production. First, GM lifted its corporate ban on 400+-ci engines in its intermediate cars, so buyers could purchase a new 1970 442 with a 455-ci V-8 straight from Oldsmobile. Or, for that matter, they could opt for a factory Buick GS455 or a Chevelle SS454. Second,

Distinctive graphics helped define all the dealer special and small manufacturer cars, from Shelby to Hurst to Yenko.

huge insurance surcharges on high-end performance cars had begun to put a crimp in the market. Ultimately, according to *The Hurst Heritage,* the car that was penciled in to be the 1970 Hurst/Olds was built by Oldsmobile as the Rallye 350, a car in the low-buck Road Runner mold.

Despite the lack of a Hurst/Olds in 1970, the company kept busy with other projects. Hurst teamed with Pontiac to build a series of upscale SSJ Grand Prixs. They remained in production from 1970 to 1972. Hurst also built a run of 503 full-size Chrysler 300 H hardtops and convertibles, and helped supply parts for AMC's Rebel "The Machine" in 1970.

An opportunity for Hurst to jump back into Oldsmobile production arose in 1972. That year, the company's bid to become the supplier of Indy 500 pace cars was accepted, and the 442 was once again the foundation. Hurst supplied dozens of "track cars" for use at Indy, and sold pace car replicas to the general public. With the stricter emission control laws in place in 1972, modifying engines was risky business, and the 1972 H/Os reflected that reality. The emphasis was more on luxury items, although the cars still came with a standard 270-horsepower 455 engine, and could be ordered with a 300-horse W-30 455.

An emphasis on luxury continued with the restyled 1973 Hurst/Olds. Still, the Hurst cars usually always incorporated some worthwhile new feature. The 1973 edition came with the new BF-Goodrich radial T/A tires, a major improvement over the older bias-ply tires. In 1974 the Hurst/Olds was once again chosen for Indy 500 pace car duties. Hurst built both Cutlasses and Delta 88 convertibles for the "500" festival parade. The 1975 H/Os were the first with the Hurst/Hatch roof panels.

The Hurst/Olds combination was a fine example of how small manufacturers were able to take ordinary musclecars and create something special, filling the niches that the factories would not. Although few in number, the Hurst Oldsmobiles were perhaps the most memorable 442s ever built.

Dealer Prep

Not everyone in the 1960s had to build their own assembly line to produce a specialty car. Crafty auto dealers found ways to have the manufacturers themselves do the hard work.

Don Yenko, propietor of Yenko Chevrolet in Cannonsburg, Pennsylvania, was more than just a mover of Detroit iron. He had made a name for himself racing in the early 1960s. With that background, it was no surprise that he sought to build a performance image for his dealership.

His first tentative steps in building cars with his own name on their flanks involved a special Yenko Corvair "Stinger" in 1965. But his best-known, and best-loved, creations were a series of 427-powered Camaros and Chevelles. As mentioned previously, GM policy did not allow its over-400-ci V-8s in its intermediate and ponycar lines, fearing a backlash from federal safety regulators and Ralph Nader-inspired safety zealots. The powerful 427 was reserved for the Corvette and full-size Impala and Biscayne.

But the arrival of the Camaro in 1967 presented too-perfect a temptation. The Camaro was handsome, yet small and relatively light. And it could be ordered with a 396-ci big-block starting midyear,

Another COPO creation, the Yenko Novas were one of the better-balanced packages to come through the system. Instead of the heavy big-block V-8, the Yenko "Deuce" was built with the Camaro Z28's high-revving LT-1 350-ci V-8, rated at 360 horsepower. The highly tuned small-block was a much better fit in the lightweight Nova than Yenko's previous effort, the 427 Nova. That combination even scared Don Yenko himself. The LT-1 Novas were also far easier to insure than the 427-powered cars.

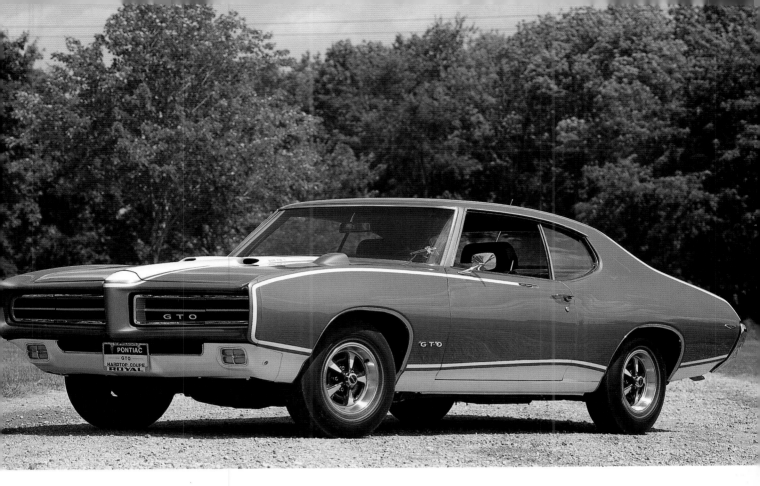

Royal Pontiac's method was to offer super-tuning services for Pontiacs, not to build their own special car. Yet their identity was as strong as many small manufacturers. And the company did build the occasional showpiece. The 1969 Royal GTO pictured was raced at the strip and along suburban Detroit's Woodward Avenue. It is equipped with the extra-rare Ram Air V V-8, a powerplant never put into production.

meaning a 427 would nestle just as snuggly between the fenders. In 1967 Yenko took 54 SS350 Camaros and swapped in 427-ci big-blocks. In 1968 the dealership started with SS396 Camaros and built 64 more 427-powered Camaros.

Yenko was not the only dealer to come to this obvious conclusion. In California, performance-minded dealer Dana Chevrolet created its own engine-swapped 427 Camaro, as did Nickey Chevrolet in Chicago. Most offered the standard Corvette 427 engine in four-barrel (425 horsepower) or three-two-barrel (435 horsepower) form, but also offered a host of aftermarket speed goodies. One dual-quad, 12.5:1 compression 427 Nickey Camaro tested by *Car and Driver* had a rating of 550 horsepower.

On the East Coast, New York speed shop Motion Performance teamed with Baldwin Chevrolet to produce their own 427 Camaros. These engine swap specials were sold only through Baldwin or Motion, and catered rather obviously to the street racing crowd. They put particular focus on solving

the Camaro's traction problems, developing their own traction bar kit and suspension package. Their standard SS427 Camaro package came with Chevy's 425-horsepower L72 V-8, but Baldwin-Motion guaranteed its top-line "Phase III" SS427 Camaros would run mid-11-second quarter miles. Baldwin-Motion was one of the most tenacious of the dealer/tuners, producing 427- and 454-powered Camaros up until 1974, when a threatening letter from the federal government finally convinced the operation to pay more attention to emission control regulations.

But swapping engines has never been the optimum scenario for car dealerships. Besides being labor intensive, it can create warranty hassles for the dealer and car buyer. And in the late 1960s, new emission control regulations raised uncomfortable legal questions about the practice.

Getting the manufacturer to build the desired engine/car combination was the best way to go, and, fortunately, GM had a backdoor for making

What good is a dealer special hot rod if nobody knows it's special? Royal Pontiac offered several forms of identification to scare off the curious.

that happen. Chevrolet had an internal ordering system for satisfying customers who needed special fleet or severe-duty vehicles. Known as the Central Office Production Order (COPO), the system was used to accommodate customers who had equipment needs beyond those offered in the standard catalog—larger station wagon brakes on a customer's fleet order of delivery sedans, for example, or perhaps a special Buick-exclusive color for an order of Chevy trucks.

The COPO system could even be used to place 427-ci V-8s in Camaros and Chevelles, if enough were ordered to justify the costs. Don Yenko's involvement was crucial in getting Chevrolet to build the 1969 427 Camaros. He convinced the division that he could sell the 500 cars Chevrolet set as a minimum to greenlight the project. Most of these cars were fitted with the L72 427, which Yenko rated at 450 horsepower, 25 horses above the stock rating. These COPO Camaros came standard with the cowl induction hood and functional fresh air inlet. Yenko replaced the stock exhaust manifolds with headers, but otherwise left the engines in factory tune. The cars were striped as "Yenko/SC" Camaros, and sold not just at Yenko Chevrolet, but through a small network of dealers nationwide.

The COPO L72 427 Camaros were not limited to Yenko. Berger Chevrolet in Grand Rapids, Michigan, Nickey and Dana Chevrolet dealerships were other outlets for the bruising ponycar. Exact numbers are sketchy, but several hundred of the cars were built.

Even rarer was the COPO/ZL-1 Camaro. The ZL-1 engine was an aluminum 427 rated at 430 horsepower, although 500 was closer to the truth. Only 69 of these ultimate Camaros were built. (Two Corvettes equipped with the ZL-1 were also produced that year.) The $4,100 price of the engine option ensured they were sold only to serious racers. Fred Gibb Chevrolet and Berger Chevrolet, catering heavily to drag racers, were the aggressors in getting the ZL-1 Camaros out.

The COPO pipeline also produced 99 427-powered Chevelles in 1969. In 1970 Yenko connected the dots to create another COPO special, a Nova powered by the Z/28 Camaro's 360-horsepower LT-1 350-ci V-8. Yenko's dealership had built a small run of 427-powered SYC Novas in 1969, which proved to be hairy enough to scare even Don Yenko himself. The LT-1 Yenko Novas were a much better-balanced package.

While the COPO ordering system was largely about helping fleet buyers order minor changes for their cars and trucks, the strength of the 427 Camaros and Chevelles has made this once-obscure internal corporate acronym a buzz word among knowledgeable car enthusiasts. Rightly or wrongly, the term "COPO" has become married to the 427 engine and its sheet metal Chevrolet hosts.

Pontiac Royalty and Fast Fords

Long before the COPO pipeline had been exploited by clever Chevrolet dealers, other auto peddlers discovered that a racing connection sells cars. Ace Wilson's Royal Pontiac in Royal Oak, Michigan, was especially adept at turning a race track presence into extra business. They fielded a number of Super Duty Pontiacs in sanctioned drag racing competition and in exhibition matches. They sponsored adman Jim Wangers' Catalina when he won the 1960 Labor Day NHRA Nationals Top Stock Eliminator trophy, Pontiac's first class win in NHRA competition.

Royal's claim to fame among the street performance crowd was its "Royal Bobcat" supertuning kits. A buyer could choose differing levels of Bobcat tuning, but the basic package consisted of rejetting the carburetors, recurving the distributor, and installing adjustable lock nuts on the rocker arms. For more serious performance, Royal milled the cylinder heads and installed thinner head gaskets in order to milk a higher compression ratio from the engine.

The dealership offered these services on the early-1960s Catalinas and Grand Prix, but the arrival of the GTO in 1964 really gave the Royal Bobcat moniker coast-to-coast fame. When *Car and Driver* magazine conducted its first track tests of the GTO in 1964, Royal was credited with supertuning the phenomenally quick test vehicles. Unknown until later years, Royal had also installed 421-ci short blocks in place of the stock 389 engines, guaranteeing good results.

Most of Pontiac's press fleet, at least the performance models, were prepped by Royal. As the resident enthusiast at Pontiac's advertising agency, Wangers was masterful at getting hot press cars into the right hands, and in steering visiting reporters into the Bobcatted GTOs, Firebirds, and Catalina 2+2s. Most of the dealers that built their own special musclecars were adept at getting press coverage in the car magazines of the day, but thanks to Wangers, Royal Pontiac was especially effective.

Although more a parts package than an actual special showroom model, the Royal Bobcat tuning package gave Royal Pontiac its own distinct image. "Royal Bobcat" stickers on a Pontiac provided bragging rights and just enough of a menacing presence to boost egos among owners.

Tasca Ford in Providence, Rhode Island, filled a similar function for Ford lovers. Bob Tasca figured early on that racing was a good way to reach young buyers. In the early-to-mid-1960s, Tasca Ford livery adorned just about every type of factory-built racing Ford, including lightweight Galaxies, Thunderbolts, and A/FX Mustangs. The performance image worked for Tasca Ford in the mid-1960s, as the dealership sold huge numbers of 427 Galaxies, Mustang GTs, and Shelbys to the general public.

Tasca Ford may be best remembered, however, for its role in creating the 428 Cobra Jet Mustang. As the 1960s marched on, and musclecars became as plentiful as Boston Celtic NBA championships, Ford's image among the street racing crowd suffered. Fords won everything in sight at the race track, sure, but those wins didn't transfer any special prowess to their offerings for the street. The 390 four-barrel V-8 and the Fairlane GT, Mercury Cyclone GT, and Mustang GT it powered were underachievers by almost any standard. As the popularity of ponycars and intermediate-sized vehicles increased, no one wanted to hear about ocean liner-sized 427 Galaxies.

One problem was interchangeability of parts, an area where Chevrolet clearly had the lead. But with Ford's steady stream of high-performance big-block engines—including the 1960 352 Special, the 1961 390 triple two-barrel V-8, the 1962 triple two-barrel 406, the red-meat 427, and the 428 Police Interceptor—the raw material was there. As *Hot Rod* writer Eric Dahlquist put it in 1968, "Ford has had the good pieces right along, but getting them into a package was the problem."

To rebuild that "Total Performance" image, not to mention moving some cars off the lot, Tasca Ford found the combination. They took a 1967 Mustang GT 390, and replaced the mediocre big-block with a Police Interceptor 428 infused with assorted 427 parts. They showed off the finished product to *Hot Rod*, prompting the magazine to conduct a poll on whether Ford should build it or not.

Ford could hardly ignore the resounding "yes." The production version was given the nonsensical name of "428 Cobra Jet," but everything else about the engine made sense. Using the previously luxury car-oriented 428 as a base, Ford added 427 low-riser

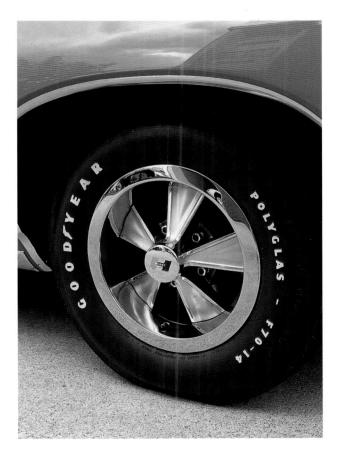

Hurst wasn't just known for the Hurst/Olds musclecars. Long before such hot rods entered the picture Hurst made a name for itself with heavy-duty shifters and attractive custom wheels such as these.

Grand Spaulding Dodge paid particular attention to the A-body Mopars, giving them a personality they sorely lacked. His GSS Darts and Demons were different almost every year. For 1971, as shown, the hook was the 340 Six Pack engine. The next year Grand Spaulding offered a supercharged 340.

cylinder heads, a performance intake manifold, a single 735 cfm Holley four-barrel carburetor, a cold air induction package, and the hydraulic lifters and cam used in the 390 GT engine. Compared with the expensive and cranky 427, the 428 Cobra Jet was a relative bargain, and tractable too. *Hot Rod* recorded a 13.56-second quarter mile at 106.64 miles per hour, and called the Cobra Jet Mustang "probably the fastest regular production sedan ever built."

Tasca Ford continued to be a master at selling both high-performance cars and a high-performance image. Another of the company's projects was an 11-second 1969 Boss 429 street car that reportedly never lost an impromptu speed challenge. Tasca also sold a small run of their own special 429 SCJ Torino Cobras in 1970, complete with headers, electric fuel pump, and a lowered nose.

Mr. Mopar

Mopar lovers had their super dealer, too. The snorting ram's head window stickers bearing the "Mr. Norm's Sport Club" and "Dyno-tuned" inscriptions were the badges worn by customers of Chicago-based Grand Spaulding Dodge. The dealership built its legend around its line of dyno-tuned musclecars and special edition Darts and Demons. The "Mr. Norm" that gave Grand Spaulding its identity was the flamboyant Norman Kraus, who never met a

promotion he didn't like when it came to selling high-performance Dodges. For a time the dealership was the number one seller of Dodge musclecars in the United States.

Grand Spaulding Dodge commanded the same sort of respect from Chrysler headquarters as Tasca Ford did from Blue Oval corporate offices. When the Dart was redesigned and enlarged for 1967, Grand Spaulding Dodge was the first to drop a 383-ci big-block between its fenders, a feat the factory engineers had thought impractical. After showing the project car to Dodge Division general manager Robert McCurry, a 383 Dart GTS option was given the green light for production, with a late 1967 introduction.

Kraus, ever the promoter, immediately concocted his own "GSS" 383 Darts. The 383 was by then a factory option for the Dart, but Mr. Norm's dealership was so successful selling its dyno-tuned GSS Darts that many people thought the 383 was an exclusive Grand Spaulding option.

Of course, the next obvious experiment was to drop the taller 440-ci big-block into the Dart, which Grand Spaulding tried in late 1967. This time, Dodge contracted with Hurst Performance Research to build the several hundred 440-powered Darts.

As with the 383, tricks required to make the 440 fit included installing a unique exhaust system, modifying the K-frame, and installing new motor mounts. Due to the height of the "RB" series 440, the engine crowded out the power brake booster, but on these types of cars "go" was given considerable priority over "stop." The muscular Darts were fairly low-key from the outside, with only "440" engine identification on the hood bulges giving away the secret. For their specials, Grand Spaulding dyno-tuned the package, added their own traction bar, and slapped on GSS badges.

For 1970 the Challenger was the big news from Dodge, so the GSS package was shifted to that model. But Grand Spaulding then went back to the A-body platform in 1971. Plymouth had scored a huge sales success with the semi-fastback Duster in 1970, so the following year Dodge got its own version, the Demon. With the 340 Demon, Grand Spaulding found a suitable home for it GSS package, and created two of the most memorable A-body Mopars ever built.

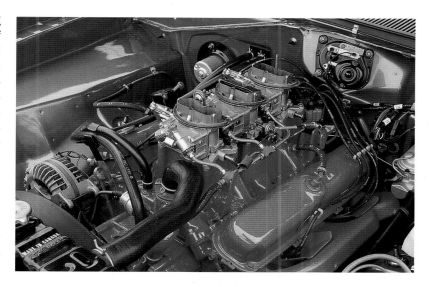

For the 1971 GSS Demons, Mr. Norm took an underused idea from Chrysler, the Six Pack induction for the 340 V-8, and made it his own. Why not? The parts, originally used on the T/A Challenger and AAR 'Cuda, were all available through normal Mopar parts channels.

The 1971 Demon GSS was sold with the 340 engine fitted with the "Six Pack" induction used on the 1970 Challenger T/A. The 340 Six Pack V-8 was a T/A and AAR 'Cuda exclusive in 1970, but all the parts for the triple Holley two-barrel setup were in the Chrysler parts catalog, waiting to be found by an enterprising dealer like Mr. Norm.

Throughout the years Grand Spaulding Dodge had campaigned a series of supercharged Mopars in drag racing competition, and for 1972 attached their name to one more supercharged project. Looking for a different angle, Kraus and company developed a Demon GSS package that featured a Paxton supercharged 340 underhood. Their timing was excellent—to run on the new unleaded gasoline and meet emission requirements, Chrysler dropped the 340's compression ratio in 1972, making a street supercharger setup feasible. The blown GSS was listed at $3,595, about $800 higher than a base Demon 340.

By 1973 most of the supercar dealers had moved on to greener pastures, or rather had been pushed on. Federal pollution controls left no room for engine swap specials, and the performance car market was drying up anyway. The Royal Pontiac team started to break apart in 1970. Tasca Ford switched to selling Lincolns and Mercurys in 1971, betting that luxury cars were the next big wave. Grand Spaulding stopped building its GSS line after 1972.

One might well wonder how dealers like Grand Spaulding, Yenko Chevrolet, Royal Pontiac, and others were able to put so many extraordinarily fast cars into the hands of so many young people, given that a lot of older teens and early twenty-somethings relied on their parents' deep pockets to finance their hot rod dreams. More than one parent looked askance at the prospect of turning loose their babies in 400-horsepower muscle machines. In a case like this it's very important to never underestimate the undaunting power of salesmanship.

"A lot of parents used to come in very leery about their kids [owning fast cars]," Kraus recalled. "I said 'You know, you're going to know your kids are gonna be in the garage working on the car late at night.'

"'You dealers will say anything to sell a car!' That was the response.

"A month later I would get a call from these people," Kraus said. "'I apologize for saying that to you. My son is in the garage every night. It is such a pleasure. He's working on the car, he's cleaning the car, his girlfriend is down there with him. And on the weekends they go out to the track and I know they aren't racing in the city.'"

Super-tuned musclecars as anti-juvenile delinquent strategy? Well, why not? It's hardly any more outrageous than most of the claims made about 1960s supercars through the years.

SUPER CARS OF THE 1980S AND 1990S

At first glance it may seem the age of factory special musclecars came to an abrupt end in the early 1970s. The decade remembered for custom vans, Ford Pintos, and Chevy Vegas was hardly a breeding ground for collectible American iron. But a handful of survivors continued to pop up throughout the 1970s, keeping momentum alive until the next musclecar revival rekindled during the 1980s. In the 1990s that flame relit at full intensity, producing cars that were every bit the equal of their 1960s counterparts. Cars like the Mustang Cobra R and ACR Viper are the modern equivalent of the lightweight Galaxies and super stock Dodges of the 1960s.

Hurst Marathon

The most prominent survivor from the bell-bottom decade was the Hurst/Olds. Although hardly the fire-breathing draggers the earlier cars were, the Hurst/Olds vehicles produced during the 1970s were indeed a cut above their pedestrian counterparts. They at least continued to offer Hurst shifters, big tires, and big engines.

As covered in chapter five, the collaboration between Hurst Performance and Oldsmobile remained more or less intact throughout the dark days of the 1970s. Some variation of the Hurst/Olds remained in continuous production from

Dodge's ACR program started modestly enough, with a Neon configured for SCCA amateur events. When the concept was applied to the Viper, you got a V-10-powered sports car supplied at the factory with racing harnesses for the seats, massive 18-inch BBS wheels and Michelin Pilot sport tires, racing springs and shock absorbers, a K&N air filter that bumped up horsepower by 10, and weight-saving equipment deletions.

As with Hurst/Olds Cutlasses from earlier times, there was no mistaking the special model for anything else. Although the 307-ci V-8 was weak by 1960s standards, it was competitive with other performance cars of the day.

1972 to 1975. The special edition Oldsmobiles served as Indy pace cars in 1972 and 1974. Some modest excitement was created in 1975, the first year the Hurst/Hatch roof panels, commonly known as T-tops, were made available. That excitement waned as the roof panels quickly earned a reputation for leaking. The Hurst/Olds could still be ordered with a 455-ci V-8, at a time when engine displacements were heading in the opposite direction.

The Hurst/Olds name returned in 1979 on the downsized Cutlass. Like most of the other Hurst specials of the 1970s, the 1979 edition was available with black or white paint schemes with gold trim. No manual transmission was available, but the TurboHydramatic transmission was controlled by a Hurst dual-gate shifter. While other Cutlass two-door coupes had the 305-ci Chevy V-8 as the top option, the Hurst edition came with an Olds "W-30" 350-ci four-barrel V-8, even if it was only rated at 170 horsepower, 10 more than the 305.

The cars were also hobbled by extremely high 2.56:1 and 2.73:1 axle ratios. Also lessening the appeal of these cars is that they were not modified at the Hurst facilities; they were built entirely on the Oldsmobile assembly lines.

The Hurst/Olds went on hiatus again after 1979, but 1983 represented a good opportunity to revive the brand since it was the 15th anniversary of the first Cutlass given the Hurst Performance treatment. The timing was opportune in other ways as well. To anyone waking up from a 15-year slumber, it must have looked, at first glance, as if the good times had never stopped: The 1983 Ford Mustang GT was released upon the world with a bulging hood scoop, Holley four-barrel carburetor atop its 302-ci V-8, and a five-speed transmission; Carroll Shelby had his name on a car again, this time a front-wheel-drive Dodge Charger; and the Camaro Z28 and Firebird Trans-Am were sleeker than ever. It was the beginning of a modest new-generation musclecar boom.

The 15th anniversary Hurst/Olds was fitted with a front air dam and rear deck spoiler. Hurst built 3,000 in 1983.

Of course, a closer examination would have revealed these cars to be much milder versions of their 1960s cousins, thanks to a decade of increasingly strict emissions laws and corporate average fuel economy requirements (although handling was much improved). And so it was with the 1983 Hurst/Olds, but the finished product was still worthwhile, and popular.

The new H/O was powered by a 307-ci Olds V-8 that produced 180 horsepower and 245 ft-lbs of torque. The engine was mildly hopped up with a long-duration camshaft and valvetrain to match, low-restriction exhaust, and Rochester 4MV Quadrajet four-barrel carburetor. A 3.73:1 axle ratio was standard, with limited slip optional. The Hurst shifters installed that year were the Lightning Rod design, an eye-catching bundle of three stalks sprouting from the center console. The rods controlled a four-speed automatic transmission.

The suspension was upgraded with high-rate springs and shocks, a 1.25-inch diameter front anti-sway bar and a .875-inch rear bar, quick-ratio steering, and Goodyear Eagle GT radials on 15x7 wheels. A nonfunctional hood scoop completed the 1960s muscle image.

The final Hurst/Olds arrived the following year. Mechanically, the 1984 edition was almost identical to the 1983 edition. Silver two-tone paint with black

lower section and red accent stripes were the obvious differences. With the 1980s version of a musclecar revival working with a rapidly improving American economy, Oldsmobile produced 3,500 Hurst/Olds Cutlasses that year, making the 1984 edition the most popular of all.

That popularity couldn't save the Hurst/Olds for the long term, however. General Motors' plans for its intermediate-sized cars included a shift to a front-wheel-drive platform, and a switch to four-cylinder and V-6 powerplants. No legitimate Hurst/Olds could be built on such a platform, at least in the eyes of enthusiasts. Oldsmobile learned this lesson the hard way when it attempted to graft the 442 nameplate onto a shrunken, four-cylinder version of the Cutlass Calais later in the decade. No one was fooled, and the act hurt Oldsmobile more than helped it. Fortunately, the Hurst/Olds legacy escaped such a fate.

Shelby Revival

Carroll Shelby's reentry into the specialty automobile game started modestly enough. Lee Iacocca, hired to turn around Chrysler Corporation's fortunes, was looking for a way to inject a little life into the company's workmanlike product offerings in the early 1980s. During his tenure at Ford Iacocca had dealt with Shelby, and the two trusted and liked

Every Hurst/Olds came with a Hurst shifter, and, in 1983, "Lightning Rods" were featured. With the Lightning rods the car could be left in drive, or the outer rods could manually shift gears from first to second and second to third. The rods commanded a four-speed automatic transmission. The feature returned in 1984.

horsepower, compared to the regular 2.2's rating of 94, thanks to an increased compression ratio, some fiddling with the cam timing, a fattened spark advance, and greater fuel flow from the Holley two-barrel carburetor. The Shelby Charger's 50-series tires helped the car achieve handling targets drivers of earlier Shelby Mustangs could only dream of.

The Shelby Charger returned in 1984, and in 1985 was upgraded through the addition of a turbocharger. The 1985 turbo 2.2 developed 146 horsepower. In 1986, however, the Shelby Dodges became something more than just production-line hatchbacks with Shelby stickers. That year Shelby opened his own production facility, Shelby Automobiles, in Whittier, California, geared toward creating limited production cars. As he had done in the 1960s with Mustangs, Shelby took delivery of partly finished cars from Chrysler and modified them extensively, giving the cars a distinct new personality.

each other. Shelby, after a decade spent big-game hunting and selling chili mixes, was ready get back into the automotive arena as well. He signed with Chrysler in 1982.

The collaboration started at the newly christened Chrysler Shelby Performance Center in Santa Fe Springs, California. Although the new cars were front-wheel driven and powered by four-cylinder engines, the early 1980s was still a time before fuel injection and extensive underhood electronics were the norm. Time-tested hot-rodding techniques, such as big cams, big carbs, and big exhaust, still applied. Most of the improvements since the 1960s had been gained in tire and handling science.

Consequently, it took a relatively short time to turn out the 1983 Shelby Dodge Charger, the first American production car to bear Shelby's name since 1970. The Shelby Charger was more Dodge than Shelby, being built on the same factory line as all the other Chargers, but it was a beginning. The Shelby's 2.2-liter four-cylinder was rated at 107

The first car to emerge from Shelby Automobiles was the 1986 Omni GLHS. The GLH (Goes Like Hell) Omni had been introduced in 1984 as a kind of bare-bones family performance car. The hot hatchback came with big tires, the Shelby Charger engine, and a low sticker price. In 1985 the GLH could be ordered with a turbocharger. The Shelby GLHS went even further, upping the turbo boost, adding an intercooler, and installing a special Shelby-designed intake manifold. Horsepower jumped to 175, and quarter-mile times plummeted to 14.9 seconds in a *Car and Driver* road test.

In 1987 Shelby copied the Omni blueprint to create a run of 1,000 GLHS Chargers. Offerings expanded to include a Shelby Lancer and Shadow CSX in 1987, a CSX-T (for Thrifty Rental) in 1988, and a Shelby Dakota and variable vane turbo CSX in 1989.

Although not traditional musclecars cast in the V-8/rear-wheel-drive mold, the Shelby Dodges were nonetheless capable performance cars. They did not race in NASCAR or make an impact in professional drag racing, but they did find a home in SCCA and IMSA sports car competition. As factory special muscle-cars go, the limited edition Shelby Dodges were right for their time.

NASCAR Matters, Again

In the time since Ford, Mercury, Dodge, and Plymouth waged their stock car battles with special long-nosed and bewinged aero cars in the late 1960s and early 1970s, NASCAR racing had grown up. Once a Southern regional sport favored by bootleggers and hot rodders, NASCAR had developed a nationwide following during the 1980s.

The first live telecast of the Daytona 500 was beamed into American homes in 1979, and the expansion of cable television and all-sports network ESPN in the 1980s provided a regular home for the once-provincial series. Drivers no longer towed their own cars to the track on the backs of open trailers. Mobile-home-sized transporters festooned with Fortune 500 logos were the norm.

In this new environment, NASCAR racing took on added importance for Detroit automakers, at least for General Motors and Ford. Chrysler dropped out of factory-backed stock car racing in the 1970s, leaving the spotlight to Ford, Chevrolet, Pontiac, and Buick.

Through most of the late 1970s and early 1980s, General Motors had its run of NASCAR, with only a few token Ford victories. Two changes in the early 1980s altered that dynamic. The first was the creation of the Special Vehicle Operations (SVO) department at Ford in 1980, headed by Michael Kranefuss. After a decade away from factory-sponsored racing, SVO was Ford's signal that its self-imposed exile was over. Ford was losing huge sums of money in a changing marketplace, and racing was once again seen as a way to attract buyers to Ford dealerships.

SVO was organized to create a wide-ranging racing program, develop racing parts and equipment, and build limited numbers of unique performance cars. Slowly, but surely, SVO's new catalog of racing parts and Ford's willingness to assist racers paid off with victories in IMSA road races, SCORE and HDRA off-road races, and NHRA and IHRA Pro Stock drag races.

The second major thorn in General Motors side was Ford's new commitment to aerodynamics in its production vehicles, specifically with its new 1983 Thunderbird. After years of building blocky and aerodynamically challenged bricks, the T-Bird was a radical break from the last ten years of Ford design

Chasing down Fords was the whole point of the "Aeroback" Monte Carlo and Grand Prix 2+2. Chevrolet put the sloping rear glass into production solely for racing purposes, namely to apply more downforce to the rear at speed. The examples shown are from the Klassix Auto Museum in Daytona Beach, Florida.

philosophy. Derided as an "egg" or "bar of soap" by its detractors, the Thunderbird bored a clean enough hole through the wind to put Ford back into the thick of NASCAR competition.

T-Bird driver Bill Elliott won 11 Winston Cup races in 1985, including the Daytona 500, the Winston 500, and the Southern 500—all the big superspeedways where aerodynamics makes a huge difference. Even though Darrel Waltrip won the series championship that year, alarm bells went off all over GM.

The response came in 1986. Even though NASCAR racing had drifted far away from its "stock car" origins, the sanctioning body still required participating cars to run stock-appearing sheet metal. That meant Chevrolet and Pontiac had to put into

production any car with drastically altered aerodynamics. And so, just as Plymouth and Dodge had released street versions of the Superbird and Charger Daytona, and Ford produced Torino Talladegas for public consumption, GM built special production versions of an "aero back" Monte Carlo SS and Pontiac Grand Prix 2+2.

The designs were quickly readied and released during the 1986 racing season. For the Monte Carlo SS, the changes were mostly limited to a sloping rear glass that smoothed the car's formal roofline. The biggest advantage of the new rear glass was to cut rear lift, giving the cars better downforce. Pontiac went a step further and grafted on a new nose to smooth out airflow, and saw the bigger aerodynamic gains of the two. The Grand Prix 2+2 remained a special edition car, but the sloping rear glass became standard Monte Carlo SS equipment in 1987.

In true factory special musclecar fashion, the huge rear glass created compromises in other areas. The glass intruded upon the size of the trunk opening, especially on the Pontiac. The 2+2's trunk opening was described as a "mail slot" by *Car and Driver*, who also couldn't help but notice the poor quality control on these special stock car editions.

Additionally, while the factory race cars of the 1960s had the beans to back up the bodywork, the 1980s-era fastbacks were more flash than dash. The Pontiac 305-ci four-barrel V-8 put out a mere 165 horsepower (later downgraded to 150), and limped through the quarter mile in 17.6 seconds at 80 miles per hour in *Car and Driver's* August 1986 tests. The Monte Carlo SS was a bit better, with 180 horsepower and a 16.8-second quarter mile, but no one mistook these cars for Talladegas or Superbirds. "The money you'll shell out for either of these speedway specials ($16,325 for the Monte, a whopping $18,214 for the Prix) will buy you a lot more automotive pleasure elsewhere," noted Rich Ceppos in *Car and Driver*.

As for Ford's response, they enjoyed needling GM. In 1986 advertising featuring Bill Elliott's No. 9 T-Bird, headlined "The Ford that changed the shape of NASCAR," ad copywriters bragged that "The

The first Shelby Dodge to emerge from the Shelby Automobiles plant in Whittier, California, was the 1986 Omni GLHS. The earlier Shelby Chargers had had their Shelby gear installed on a regular Dodge production line. Although derived from a pedestrian FWD econobox, the GLHS had a fantastic power-to-weight ratio thanks to the Shelby modifications. Published reports recorded 14.9-second quarter miles.

119

Ford built the 1993 Cobra R for sanctioned competition, although many of the factory-racer Mustangs were quietly shuffled off to private collections, the better to appreciate in value. This example, shown at the 1994 Dallas Grand Prix, is serving its intended purpose.

tremendous success of the Thunderbird last year helps to explain why the competition has brought a whole flock of radically redesigned cars to the NASCAR Winston Cup circuit this year.

"Their purpose: to try and match the aerodynamics, speed and handling already found in the Thunderbird," the ad read. "And perhaps the best accolade of all is the acknowledgment by the competition that they needed to go back to the drawing board."

Ford's bravado notwithstanding, the aero-back Monte Carlo kept Chevy at the front of the standings. After Ford's breakthrough year in 1985, Chevy drivers won 18 of 29 races in 1986 and 15 of 30 in 1987. Results for Pontiac were not so encouraging, with 2 wins each in 1986 and 1987, although to be fair, there were fewer Pontiac teams in competition. The aero-back SS Montes and 2+2 Grand Prixs may not have been the hottest or best-looking cars on the street, but they did their jobs on the track, which was the whole point.

Fixing the Camaro and Firebird

Ford caused General Motors problems in other areas as well. During the 1980s the 5.0-liter Mustang GT evolved into *the* musclecar of the decade. While the Camaro and Firebird had sleek looks and a handling advantage, the 5.0-liter Mustang had the more important qualities—cheaper and faster.

Chevrolet sought to neutralize that advantage in a number of ways, one of which was to emphasize the Camaro's handling advantages in road racing competition. By the late 1980s the SCCA Trans-Am series had shifted far away from its production car-based origins into silhouette bodies and tube-frame chassis territory. The new home for more-or-less stock ponycars was in the SCCA Escort Endurance, Canadian Players' Challenge, and IMSA Firehawk series.

With an eye toward improving the on-track performance of the Camaro, Chevrolet released a small run of "1LE" Camaros in 1988. The 1LE option, in

Although its engine earned no plaudits, the thinking behind the Pontiac Grand Prix 2+2 was the same as that behind the Dodge Daytona Charger and Ford Talladega; namely, build a street car with specific aerodynamic enhancements that could be used to improve the car's performance in NASCAR. The bubbleback rear glass and sloping nosepiece were unique to the 2+2. *Pontiac Historic Services*

time-honored factory race car tradition, reduced vehicle weight through the elimination of air conditioning and heating, fog lamps, and the substitution of an aluminum driveshaft for the standard piece. The 1LE Camaros came standard with four-wheel disc brakes, and the option was tied to a performance rear axle. The 305-ci V-8 and the 350 could be teamed with 1LE gear.

A relatively low-profile project as far as the general public was concerned, the 1LE Camaros nonetheless got the job done on the race track. Production peaked in 1992 at 705 units, although the option continued to be offered on the next generation E-body introduced in 1993.

The 1LE option helped polish the Camaro's race track reputation, but the Mustang GT continued to

be the car to beat on the street in the early 1990s. The Mustang regularly outsold both the Camaro and Firebird combined. The GM F-bodies jumped into the street performance lead in 1993, however, due to the strength of the redesigned Camaro and Firebird and their 275-horsepower LT-1 5.7-liter V-8s. The 1993 Mustang GT carried the same 225 horsepower rating it had for years, and even the new Cobra, with its 245 horses, was outclassed by the F-bodies. Aggressive pricing by General Motors put the Camaro and Mustang on equal footing.

As the F-bodies enjoyed a performance resurgence, special edition models were bound to follow. The most successful of these were produced by SLP engineering (motto: "increased performance with emissions compliance"). The GM/SLP cars were

The whole philosophy behind SLP engineering was street legal performance, so engine modifications have usually been limited to Ram Air induction systems and cat-back exhaust. But even those modest pieces, when combined with the SLP suspension and rear-end options, make for a performance car on par with any from the 1960s. Shown is the 1998 Trans-Am Firehawk.

shipped from GM facilities to SLP engineering, where the specialty company performed the modifications. The first collaboration between GM and SLP was the Firebird Firehawk introduced in 1992. Given SLP's dedication to legal performance, engine modifications were few, but did include a functional cold air induction package and a cat-back exhaust system. The earlier generation car was also given larger wheels and tires and better brakes, plus unique spoilers. Only 25 were built, but it was a start.

When the new generation Firebirds arrived there was much more raw material to work with, and each year brought new upgrades. By 1994 the fully optioned Firehawk produced 300 horsepower. In 1995 a Hurst shifter was added to the option list, and SLP advertised quarter-mile times of 13.5 seconds at 103.5 miles per hour. Offerings expanded to include a Comp T/A. In 1996, "high-flow" exhaust manifolds bumped horsepower to 310. In 1997 SLP built a special run of 29 LT-4 powered Firehawks, rated at 330 horsepower. In 1998 the standard LS1 V-8 was rated at 327 horsepower. In previous years the Firehawks were all based on the Formula model, but the equipment could be ordered on the Trans-Am starting in 1998.

The relationship between General Motors and SLP proved solid enough that Chevrolet got into the game in 1996. Reaching back into the division's past, Chevrolet named its SLP special the Z28 SS.

The Z28 SS was hard to miss—its most prominent feature was a large, functional hood scoop. The 17x9-inch wheels and 40-series rubber, along with modest suspension modifications, enhanced the Camaro's already-superior handling. With the optional free-flow exhaust, horsepower hit 310. By 1999 that had risen to 327 on the top option Z28 SS.

These special editions helped vault the Camaro and Firebird ahead of the Mustang in useable street performance, if not in sales. Not since the 1960s had so much power been available to pony-car buyers.

SVO, SVT, and Cobra R

Keeping track of all the high-performance Mustangs produced from 1982 to 2000 is no easy task. There have been 5.0-liter GTs, Turbo GTs, 20th anniversary GT-350s, and LX 5.0-liters. But the most noteworthy late-model Mustangs have come from either Ford's in-house performance group, or a small group of latter-day Shelbys such as Saleen or Steeda.

When Ford established the SVO division in 1980, its primary mission was to get Ford's new racing program revved up and on a winning foot. But it was also tasked with creating specialty vehicles that were difficult to integrate into Ford's mass production systems geared toward spitting out millions of cars and trucks every year.

SVO's first project was the aptly named 1984 SVO Mustang. As a performance car, it was definitely a product of its times. Most automotive seers at the time believed the traditional V-8 engine was on its way toward extinction, after two oil crises in the 1970s and stricter federal Corporate Average Fuel Economy (CAFE) requirements in the 1980s. Across the industry, engineering resources were focused on hot four-cylinder and six-cylinder projects.

At Ford, that meant the newest hot Mustang came to market with a four-cylinder foundation. But the SVO edition was truly something special, a breakthrough for the Mustang line. Its 2.3-liter OHC four-cylinder was fuel-injected, turbocharged, and intercooled, and produced 175 horsepower. The advanced electronics allowed a cockpit-mounted switch that altered ignition timing so the SVO could run on either regular or premium fuel. The SVO came with four-wheel disc brakes and the largest tires ever fitted to a Mustang. Its memorable outward characteristics included an offset hood scoop and a large double-wing rear spoiler.

In its short life the SVO Mustang was upgraded considerably. By its final year, 1986, the SVO sported true dual exhaust and 200 horsepower.

In many ways the SVO was arguably the best performance Mustang ever built to that point, if all-

around ability is taken into account. But the expected demise of the V-8 never occurred, and the 5.0-liter GT was also upgraded throughout the 1980s. The SVO was burdened by a pricier window sticker and a slower elapsed time than the 5.0-liter GT.

Shortly before the launch of the next genuinely special Mustang, the Cobra, in 1993, Ford's SVO department was turned upside down. What emerged was the Special Vehicle Team (SVT), which was tasked specifically with designing and building limited-run, specialty niche vehicles. The first fruit of SVT's labor was the Mustang Cobra and F-150 Lightning. The Lightning was a hot rod truck, powered by a special, very stout 351W that produced 245 horsepower. The kick in the seat was noteworthy, but the Lightning's ability to turn a corner was what really impressed lucky drivers.

Trading on a name from Ford's past, the Mustang Cobra was indeed a higher-performance car than the GT, but the Cobra was about more than just power. By 1993 the Mustang in general, and the car's suspension in particular, felt like relics from another era. The Fox-chassis Mustang traced its roots to the 1978 Fairmont, hardly a high-performance platform. With a surplus of power, a live rear axle, and a MacPherson strut front end, the Mustang rode on a less sophisticated suspension than

The prominent feature of the SLP-produced Camaro Z28 SS is the center-mounted hood scoop, which supplies the engine with cold air. The SS tag first reappeared in 1996; shown is the 1998 model.

With the Mustang Cobra R series, built in 1993, 1995, and 2000 (shown), Ford has returned to the days of factory-built race cars. The race-tuned engine, sky-high wing, and massive hood bulge recall the days of lightweight Galaxies and Thunderbolts. *SVT photo*

even some of the cheapest Japanese imports—not to mention the all-new Camaro. With the Cobra, Ford sought to soften those rough edges.

The Cobra actually employed softer rear coil springs, softer shocks and struts, and smaller front anti-roll bar. But the softer suspension, in conjunction with the 17-inch wheels and 245-series tires, actually improved handling abilities. With the new parts the Mustang was less prone to jitterbugging across rough pavement, allowing the suspension to make the most of the fat tires.

The Special Vehicle Team had another project in the works, however. If the 5.0-liter Mustang was the king of the street and grass roots drag racing, it left something to be desired in road racing competition. With that deficiency in mind, Ford quietly released a batch of 107 "Cobra R" Mustangs in April 1993. Ford started taking orders on April 15th. Production began on the 26th. The release of these cars was low-key because Ford hoped the R-models would end up in the possession of actual racers, rather than in collectors' garages.

These special racing Mustangs were the spiritual descendents of the lightweight Galaxies and Super

Stock Mustangs of the 1960s. As factory racers built with the SCCA World Challenge and IMSA Firehawk series in mind, the Cobra R was sold stripped-down to reduce weight and cut complexity. The rear seats, belts, sound deadener, carpeting, and inner fenders were removed. Obviously there was no radio, air conditioning, or power window equipment.

The engine was the stock Cobra 245-horsepower 5.0-liter V-8, but it was readied for racing with both an oil cooler and power steering cooler, and an aluminum two-core radiator. The suspension used stiff, variable rate springs, adjustable Koni struts and shocks, a fatter front sway bar, and a strut tower brace. In a much-needed braking improvement, the R-model came standard with vented, 13-inch front discs, and 10.5-inch rear discs. The black 17x8-inch wheels were shod with 245/45ZR17 Goodyear Gatorbacks. All the R-models were red. The R-model equipment listed for $7,205, a considerable percentage of a Mustang's sticker price.

If it seemed the Cobra R was the product of an earlier generation, a few details brought the observer back to the present. Strict federal rules required that the racing models be sold with all mandated safety and emission control equipment intact, including the airbag and catalytic converters.

How did the Cobra R fare at the track? The record was mixed. Some teams, like the Florida-based Steeda Autosports did well, but the R-model was still a step behind in many areas. And many a Cobra R did end up in collector garages.

The next racing Cobra was much more serious. The first deficiency addressed was under the hood. In a move many Mustang enthusiasts had begged for almost since the first 5.0 hit the streets, Ford slipped a 351 Windsor rated at 300 horsepower into the 1995 Cobra R. The R was also fitted with a larger fuel tank, extending that car's range. All of the 1995 R-models were painted white, with a prominent hood bulge being the other noticeable feature. Increased production of 250 helped put the 1995 R-models in the hands of more racers.

Unlike the more street friendly SVT Cobra, the Cobra R was not built every year. John Colletti, Ford Special Vehicle Engineering manager, explained the rational in a Cobra R press release: "This is the kind of car you *want* to do, when it's time," he said. "We have a simple rule of thumb for when it's time to develop a new Cobra R: first, when there's a need, and second, when the new one will be able to far outshine the old one."

Those conditions arose in 2000, and the result was a new Cobra R that made even the Boss 429 look tame. The 2000 R-model used a 5.4-liter DOHC

With a rear wing not too dissimilar from the one used on the 1970 Plymouth Superbird, the 2000 Cobra R has brought the idea of a factory-built race car full circle. The Cobra R's 385-horsepower 5.4-liter V-8 is every bit the equal of the powerplants from the musclecar era—if not superior.

version of Ford's modular V-8, tweaked to produce 385 horsepower and 385 ft-lbs of torque. The engines were hand-built at Ford's Engine Manufacturing Development Operations.

Although street Mustangs were powered by similar 4.6-liter overhead cam engines, dropping in the 5.4 was no direct swap. The Cobra R was fitted with new engine mounts and a lowered crossmember. Heads were special to the R model. "They're similar to the 4.6 Cobra heads, but with a lot more flow through the intake and exhaust ports," said Ed Olin, systems engineer at Ford's Advanced powertrain Engineering. Peak airflow was up more than 25 percent beyond the 4.6 Cobra's cylinder head, thanks to upgrades such as 2mm larger exhaust valves.

Internal engine parts included a forged crankshaft, Carrillo billet steel connecting rods, forged aluminum pistons, a Canton Racing oil pan, and a new crankshaft vibration damper. The compression ratio was 9.6:1.

Upon opening the hood, it was hard to miss the large two-piece, low-restriction intake manifold. It was mated to a larger, single-bore version of the regular Cobra's dual-bore throttle body. Exhaust manifolds were tubular steel short-tube headers connected to a Bassani X-pipe with stock Cobra catalytic converters. The 2000 Cobra R came with a Tremec T-56 manual transmission, making it the first production Mustang blessed with a six-speed tranny. Top speed was listed at over 170 miles per hour.

Like the earlier R-models, the 2000 edition was available in only one color, which was red. Only 300 examples were built, during March 2000. At this writing the 2000 R-model's racing legacy has yet to be written, but as a factory special musclecar it can already stand with any of the lightweight, swiss-cheesed, aero-nosed, bespoilered race cars Detroit built in the glory days of the 1960s.

Appendix A:

Production Figures, Factory Special Musclecars

AMC

1969 AMC/Hurst SC/Rambler	1,512
1969 SS/AMX	52
1970 Rebel "The Machine"	2,326

Chevrolet Impala Z11

1962 and 1963	57

Chevrolet Camaro Z/28 production 1967–1969 (with 302-ci V-8)

1967	602
1968	7,199
1969	20,302

Chevrolet COPO/ZL1 aluminum 427 Camaro production

1969	69

Chevrolet Camaro Indy Pace Car Production

1967	100*
1969	3,675
1982	6,360
1993	633

* No replicas built. The figure shown is the best estimate of festival cars later sold to the public.

Dodge Challenger T/A

1970	2,399

Dodge Charger 500

1969	392

Dodge Charger Daytona

1969	503

Dodge Super Stock Hemi Dart

1968	(approximately) 80

Ford 427 Thunderbolt

1964	100

Ford Lightweight Galaxies

1962	11
1963	(approximately) 200
1964	50

Ford Torino Talladega

1969	(approximately) 745

Ford Mustang, Super Stock 428 CJ

1968	50

Ford Mustang Boss 302 production

1969	1,628
1970	7,013

Ford Mustang Boss 429 production

1969	857
1970	499

Ford Mustang Cobra R production

1993	107
1995	250
2000	300

Hurst/Olds

1968	515
1969	906
1972	629
1973	1,097
1974	1,900
1975	2,535
1979	2,499
1983	3,000
1984	3,500

Plymouth Super Stock Hemi Barracuda

1968	(approximately) 70

Plymouth AAR 'Cuda

1970	2,724

Plymouth Superbird

1970	1,935

Pontiac Trans-Am

1969	697
1970	3,196

Shelby Mustangs

1965 GT350	561
1965 GT350R	36
1966 GT350	2,378

Shelby Dodge Production

1986 Omni GLHS	500
1987 Charger GLHS	1,000
1987 CSX	750
1987 Shelby Lancer	780
1988 CSX-T	999
1989 Shelby Dakota	1,490
1989 CSX	498

Appendix B:

Indy Pace Cars, 1960–2000

1960	Oldsmobile Ninety-Eight		1981	Buick Regal V-6
1961	Ford Thunderbird		1982	Chevrolet Camaro Z28
1962	Studebaker		1983	Buick Riviera convertible
1963	Chrysler 300		1984	Pontiac Fiero
1964	Ford Mustang		1985	Oldsmobile Calais
1965	Plymouth Sport Fury		1986	Chevrolet Corvette
1966	Mercury Comet Cyclone GT		1987	Chrysler LeBaron
1967	Chevrolet Camaro SS		1988	Oldsmobile Cutlass Supreme
1968	Ford Torino GT		1989	Pontiac Trans-Am Turbo
1969	Chevrolet Camaro SS		1990	Chevrolet Beretta
1970	Oldsmobile 442		1991	Dodge Viper RT/10
1971	Dodge Challenger		1992	Cadillac Allante
1972	Hurst/Olds 442		1993	Chevrolet Camaro Z28
1973	Cadillac Eldorado		1994	Ford Mustang Cobra
1974	Hurst/Olds Cutlass		1995	Chevrolet Corvette
1975	Buick Century Custom "Free Spirit"		1996	Dodge Viper GTS
1976	Buick Turbo V-6		1997	Oldsmobile Aurora
1977	Oldsmobile Delta 88		1998	Chevrolet Corvette
1978	Chevrolet Corvette		1999	Chevrolet Monte Carlo
1979	Ford Mustang		2000	Oldsmobile Aurora
1980	Pontiac Trans-Am Turbo			

Index